Self
Esteem

Self Esteem

The
New Reformation

Robert H. Schuller

WORD BOOKS
PUBLISHER
WACO, TEXAS

SELF-ESTEEM: THE NEW REFORMATION

Unless otherwise indicated, Scripture quotations are from The Revised
Standard Version of the Bible (RSV), copyright © 1946, 1952, © 1971
and 1973 by the Division of Christian Education of the National Coun-
cil of the Churches of Christ in the U.S.A.

Other Scripture quotations in this publication are from the following
sources:
   The New English Bible (NEB), © 1961, 1970 The Delegates of the
Oxford University Press and The Syndics of the Cambridge University
Press.
   The Living Bible, Paraphrased (TLB), copyright © 1971 by Tyndale
House Publishers, Wheaton, Illinois.
   The New International Version of the Bible (NIV), published by the
Zondervan Corporation, copyright © 1978 by the New York Interna-
tional Bible Society.
   The New King James Bible—New Testament (NKJV), copyright ©
1979, Thomas Nelson, Inc., Publishers
   The King James Version of the Bible (KJV).

The quotations on pages 17–18 and 19–20 are from *Celebration of Life*
by Rene Dubos. Copyright © 1981 by Rene Dubos. Used by permission
of McGraw-Hill Book Company.

Library of Congress Cataloging in Publication Data
Schuller, Robert Harold.
   Self-esteem, the new reformation.

   Includes bibliographical references.
   1. Self-love (Theology)   2. Pastoral psychology.
I. Title.
BV4639.S3458   1982   248.4   82-8356
ISBN 0–8499–0299–1   AACR2

Dedicated
to
the late
JOHN R. MULDER, D.D.
Professor of Systematic Theology
Western Theological Seminary
Holland, Michigan

Whose lectures and life
pointed me in the direction to see
the dignity in every person

Contents

Acknowledgments

MY GRATITUDE TO the faculty and student body of Western Theological Seminary in Holland, Michigan, for inviting me to first share publicly the essence of these pages in lectures at Mulder Chapel on March 4, 1982 in Holland, Michigan. And encouraging me in this publishing venture;

To Martin Marty who agreed to serve as my mentor critiquing this manuscript and being, in the process, of inestimable professional help;

To Jeanne Schuller and Sheila Coleman for their strength and assistance along the way;

To Barbara Hagler for preparing my often illegible scribble into a typed manuscript;

To *Psychology Today* and *U.S. News and World Report* for permission to quote from their publications;

To Harper and Row for permission to quote from *Stronger Than Steel: The Wayne Alderson Story* by R. C. Sproul.

My thanks to all.

Introduction

A LEADING PSYCHIATRIST and a leading churchman have shared two interesting views on this book. My friend, Dr. David Burns, Associate Professor of Psychiatry at the University of Pennsylvania,[1] wrote me:

> Dear Dr. Schuller,
> I have been reviewing with great interest your new book, *Self Esteem: The New Reformation.* . . . It is surprising how our minds have come to a similar position—you have pursued a religious route and I have pursued a scientific path, and we have both arrived at the same bottom line: unconditional self-esteem. Self-love that doesn't have to be earned because it is given.
> I believe that the vision that forms the core of most religious thinking has to do with joy. Unfortunately, the message gets distorted into fear, guilt, and mistrust. From a psychiatric point of view, I would say man's deepest flaw is to mistrust himself and to withhold love and self-acceptance. . . .
> What is exciting is that we have an impressive body of scientific research by top academicians that confirms this basic theory about depression and self-esteem. Perhaps we are at an era where psychiatric and religious thinking can be synergistic. . . .

Meanwhile, a wise scholar, Dr. Martin Marty, who kindly critiqued this manuscript said, "Is not this a philosophy which makes room for God more than a theology that incorporates psychology?" To which I replied, "Perhaps. I wouldn't be surprised. My ministry has, for over thirty years, been a mission to the unbelievers. If I were a churchman talking to church leaders, I would agree that the theocentric approach is the right approach. However, I have seen my calling as one that communicates spiritual reality to the unchurched who may not be ready to believe in God. I have been trying to carry on a dialogue with persons who are not at all prepared to listen to 'someone with God-talk.' As a missionary, I find the hope of respectful contact is based on a 'human-need' approach rather than a theological attack."

It is precisely at this point that I feel the church must be reformed. For the church to address the unchurched with a theocentric attitude is to invite failure in mission. The non-churched who have no vital belief in a relationship with God will spurn, reject, or simply ignore the theologian, church spokesperson, preacher, or missionary who approaches with Bible in hand, theology on the brain and the lips, and expects nonreligious persons to suspend their doubts and swallow the theocentric assertions as fact. The unconverted will, I submit, take notice when I demonstrate genuine concern about their needs and honestly care about their human hurts.

For decades now we have watched the church in Western Europe and in America decline in power, membership, and influence. I believe that this decline is the result of our placing theocentric communications above the meeting of the deeper emotional and spiritual needs of humanity. We have been a church first and a mission second.

The scales must tip the other way. It was appropriate for Calvin and Luther to think theocentrically. After all, "Everyone was in the church" and the issues were theological, not philosophical. For them, the central issue was, "What is the truth in theology?" The reformers didn't have to impress the unchurched so there was no need for them to take the "human needs" approach. They were a church after all, not a mission. They would "proclaim the Word of the Lord," and all had better listen!

Time and history have changed all that. Today the sincere, Christian believer is a minority. So the church must be willing to die as a church and be born again as a mission. We cannot speak out with a "Thus saith the Lord" strategy when we are talking to people who couldn't care less about the Lord! We cannot start with "What does the text say?" if we're talking to persons who aren't about to affirm respect for or unquestioning obeisance to "the text."

If we hope as a church to survive, we must learn to think and feel and talk as caring believers who are sincerely interested in understanding and meeting the deepest spiritual and emotional needs of the unbelievers. Missionaries found out long ago that the humane approach was to send out medical missionaries, linguists, and agricultural experts along with theologians. Together they approached the unbelieving community with compassion.

However, the Western church saw itself as a "church," enjoying such proud structural statements as great cathedrals and churches on mainstreets—all with social prestige. The church in America and Europe did not have to really care about the deep needs of the nonchurched. It was a successful church, and in this success the seed of death was planted. For no success is certain or stable until and unless and as long as it is committed to meeting human needs.

Those "churches" that are willing to become "missions" will succeed. Churches that are incapable of understanding what it means to become a mission, or are unwilling to pay the high price of dying as a church and being born again as a mission, will disappear entirely or will perpetuate themselves as fringe elements that are largely ignored.

This means that the most important question facing the church is: "What are the deepest needs felt by human beings?" Religious institutions who ignore this question will remain what they are—dying churches. Religious institutions that will face this question will undergo a profound revolution in the substance, strategy, style, and spirit of their ministry. And they will prosper!

Because my interest has been to succeed as a missionary for Christ to unchurched persons, I have been focusing my research and study for thirty years on discovering the deepest human need.

As I write this book, where am I coming from? I am coming out of decades of research and study of the regions of the human heart and soul.

I am convinced that the deepest of all human needs is salvation from sin and hell. I see sin as all-pervasive in humanity, infecting all human behavior and polluting the social institutions and systems at every level. The result of sin is death and hell. I perceive the agony of human distance from God and helplessness to be more profound than articulated by classical churchmen. As a result, I see what Paul Tillich calls "The demonic pervading the structures of existence." I accept the anguish of what Reinhold Niebuhr called "Systemic Evil."

We come now to the problem of semantics.

What do I mean by sin? Answer: Any human condition or act that robs God of glory by stripping one of his children of their right to divine dignity.

I could offer another complementing answer, "Sin is that deep lack of trust that separates me from God and leaves me with a sense of shame and unworthiness."

I can offer still another answer: "Sin is any act or thought that robs myself or another human being of his or her self-esteem." And what is "hell"? It is the loss of pride that naturally follows separation from God—the ultimate and unfailing source of our soul's sense of self-respect. "My God, my God, why hast thou forsaken me?" was Christ's encounter with hell. In that "hellish" death our Lord experienced the ultimate horror—humiliation, shame, and loss of pride as a human being. A person is in hell when he has lost his self-esteem. Can you imagine any condition more tragic than to live life and eternity in shame?

I must admit that I am not totally happy with that word, "Self-Esteem." Years ago I tried the word, "Self-Love." I found the pervasiveness of a negative self-image so saturated the minds of persons that most people couldn't handle that term "Self-Love." I have tried others, "Self-Worth," "Self-Dignity," "Self-Value," "Human Dignity," "Positive Self-Image," "Ego-Needs," "Human Pride," and none are perfect. I can find fault with all words. I have chosen the term "Self-Esteem" simply because I find that it becomes a philosophical bridge on which to build dialogue with other disciplines that deal with the human being: educators, psychologists, criminologists, sociologists. Let me define the term as I use it: *Self-esteem is the human hunger for the divine dignity that God intended to be our emotional birthright as children created in his image.*

I contend that this unfulfilled need for self-esteem underlies every human act, both negative and positive. Every analysis of social or personal sins must recognize that the core of all sinful or unsocial behavior is a conscious or subconscious attempt to feed the person's need for self-esteem.

Any analysis of "sin" or "evil" or "demonic influence" or "negative thinking" or "systemic evil" or "antisocial behavior" that fails to see the lack of self-dignity as the core of the problem will prove to be too shallow.

What is anger? What is hatred? It is really fear. And what is fear? It is the feeling of being threatened—a deeper feeling of insecurity. And what is that feeling of insecurity? It is a lack of self-confidence to cope with the "threatening" situation. And what is that lack of self-confidence? It is the *result* of a too-low self-esteem. "I don't think I can" rises from the deeper, "I don't think I am."

What is "lack of faith?" It is really a profoundly deep sense of unworthiness. It is a lack of trust, a projection of a deep inner insecurity. So the "unsaved" will be incapable of belief in "salvation by grace." The unsaved person cannot perceive himself as worthy of "divine grace" and hence rejects it. So salvation or the acceptance of God's forgiving grace will require a miraculous intervention of the Holy Spirit.

What does it mean to be "unloving"? This is the result of a too low self-worth. It takes, after all, a lot of faith to love!

Non-self-loving persons do not dare to love. They are afraid they'll be spurned and rejected. Why do they have that fear? Because they do not trust themselves or rate themselves high enough to believe they'll be "loved." And why do they *fear* rejection? Because rejection will only pour salt in the wounds, proving to be the straw that breaks the camel's back, as it further fuels and feeds their low self-esteem!

What is "egotism"? It is the crass and crude attempt of self-esteem-impoverished persons to "prove that they're somebody!" The truly self-esteem-satisfied persons are not "egotistic." They don't need to be.

Why is this need for self-esteem so all-consuming in individual behavior and so all-important? It is because we are made in the image of God! We were spiritually designed to enjoy the honor that befits a Prince of Heaven. We lost that position and privilege when our first parents divorced themselves from the Creator God. Many years ago a classical student of the Scriptures, Matthew Henry, in his commentaries noted on Genesis, chapter three: "The immediate consequences of Adam and Eve's transgression: Shame and fear came into the world . . . they saw themselves disrobed of all their ornaments and ensigns of honor, degraded from their dignity, and disgraced in the highest degree, laid open to the contempt and reproach of heaven and earth and their own consciences."

How human beings handle that hunger for glory explains all psychological problems, all spiritual sicknesses.

and all human sin. And this pitiful reaction to our personal need for divine dignity is profoundly pervasive.

The church must come to first understand and then meet this human need in a mission of mercy. I found myself immediately attracted to Pope John Paul II when, upon his election to the Papacy, his published speeches invariably called attention to the need for recognizing the dignity of the human being as a child of God. Recognizing this need and responding with compassion is what I'm advocating when I plead the case in this imperfect title *Self-Esteem: The New Reformation.*

During the writing of this manuscript, I commissioned George Gallup Jr., of the Gallup organization, to conduct a poll on the self-esteem of the American public today.

As might be expected, the poll conclusively demonstrated that people with a strong sense of self-esteem demonstrate the following qualities:

1. They have a high moral and ethical sensitivity.
2. They have a strong sense of family.
3. They are far more successful in interpersonal relationships.
4. Their perspective of success is viewed in terms of interpersonal relationships, not in crass materialistic terms.
5. They're far more productive on the job.
6. They are far lower in incidents of chemical addictions. (In view of the fact that current research studies show that 80 percent of all suicides are related to alcohol and drug addiction, this becomes terribly significant.)
7. They are more likely to get involved in social and political activities in their community.
8. They are far more generous to charitable institutions and give far more generously to relief causes.

In summary, the people with a positive self-esteem demonstrate the qualities of personal character that the church would happily point to with pride in the members that we develop within our institutions.

Unfortunately, the poll makes undeniably clear that the churches do not contribute to the self-esteem of persons. Only 35 percent of Protestants interviewed reflected a strong self-esteem. Thirty-nine percent of Catholics interviewed demonstrated a strong self-esteem. In the "other faiths" category, 40 percent of those interviewed demonstrated a strong self-esteem.

Obviously, the church is missing the mark.

Now, the poll makes it clear that people who view God as a personal, loving, and forgiving Being, and relate to Him in such a personal way, do develop a strong sense of self-esteem that is exceptionally high and healthy! At the same time, the poll demonstrated that ritualistic attendance at typical church services and the formal recitation of prayers do not in themselves contribute to a positive self-esteem. The facts are clear. The church is failing at the deepest level to generate within human beings that quality of personality that can result in the kinds of persons that would make our world a safe and sane society. The church is in need of a real re-reformation!

Rene Dubos, widely recognized as one of the twentieth century's great sociobiologists, made a perceptive observation in his widely acclaimed book entitled *Celebration of Life*.[2] The scientist begins with these two provocative sentences. "The most distressing aspect of the modern world is not the gravity of its problems: There have been worse problems in the past. It is the dampening of the human spirit that causes many people, especially in the countries of Western civilization, *to lose their pride in being human and to doubt that we will be able to cope* with our problems and those of the future." I applaud this analysis.

In other words, if we lose our self-esteem, we will cease to be possibility thinkers. I agree with Dubos that the human race faces problems today that finds itself on the edge of

catastrophe. Dr. Dubos continues: "There are great tragedies in the world today. Paradoxically, however, much of
contemporary gloom originates not from the difficulties we
are actually experiencing but from disasters that have not
yet happened, and may never happen. We are profoundly
disturbed by the possibility of nuclear warfare and of serious accidents in nuclear reactors. We are disturbed by the
unproven hypothesis that the widespread use of fluorocar-
bons from spray cans will damage the ozone layer and
thereby expose us to dangerous levels of ultraviolet radia-
tion. We are collectively worried because we expect that
world conditions will deteriorate if population and technol-
ogy continue growing at the present rate. The earth will
soon be overpopulated and its resources depleted; there
will be catastrophic food shortages; pollutants will rot our
lungs, dim our vision, poison us, alter the climate, and spoil
the environment. The spread of income between the have
and have-not nations will widen even further. This will
certainly increase terrorism and may eventually lead to the
use of nuclear weapons, if only as a form of blackmail." Dr.
Dubos goes on to say: "Our form of technical civilization
will eventually collapse if present trends continue. But what
a big 'if' this is. Humans aren't likely to stay passive in
dangerous situations."

Self-esteem then, or "pride in being a human being," is
the single greatest need facing the human race today. Our
very survival "as a species depends on hope. And without
hope we will lose the faith that we can cope."

Why have we lost our pride in being human? I submit
that on the deepest level this condition of lost pride is the
presence of an all-pervasive sin.

Too often, the church has contributed to the problem.
Yes, in Western civilization we have failed to distinguish
between positive pride and negative pride. Negative pride
is that destructive arrogance that assumes, "I can do anything all by myself!" It is the exact opposite of that healthy

humility I choose to call "self-esteem." Positive pride is that creative and compassionate confidence Christ inspired when he said, "You are the light of the world!" Saint Paul expressed this positive pride when he said, "I can do all things through Christ who strengthens me."

Our failure to make this distinction between positive pride and negative pride has had incredible repercussions in the church in Western Europe and in the United States. In fact, we may be touching on the single most significant cause of the decline of the church in Europe and America.

A young man in his thirties who really reflects positive pride, a healthy self-esteem, and a Christian dignity lamented to me recently, "The first nine years of my life I was a Roman Catholic. Then I became a Methodist. Next I joined a Baptist church. And from there I moved in charismatic circles. And in every one of those scenes I heard pride condemned, and I was made to feel that I was a sinner unless and until I started condemning myself.

"I started to hate myself. I lost all sense of self-esteem. Then I had an encounter with Christ. I was born again! And he didn't tell me how bad I was. I knew that and Christ knew I knew it! He just told me how great I was going to become as we walked on through life together!

"I'm really proud, and yet completely humble," he added, quoting now from the Gospel of John, "You did not choose me, but I chose you" (John 15:16), and "I am the vine, you are the branches. He who abides in me, and I in him, he it is that bears much fruit" (John 15:5).

When a human being's self-esteem is stimulated and sustained (like a branch in the trunk of a tree) in a redemptive relationship with Christ, we are truly saved from sin and hell.

In concluding his arguments on this subject, Dr. Dubos writes, "This is not the best of times, but it is nevertheless a time for celebration because, even though we realize our insignificance as parts of the cosmos and as individual members of the human family, we know that each one of us can develop a persona that is unique, yet remains part of the cosmic and human order of things. Human beings have been and remain uniquely creative because they are able to integrate the pessimism of intelligence with the optimism of will."

I would add to "the optimism of will": the power of faith!

This, of course, is not a debate; it's a decision. Years ago in a dialogue with my dear friend, philosopher, and architect, Richard Neutra, Dr. Dubos said, "If I were to be a pessimist, it would be because I see that the human being does have a strong inclination to adjust—downward." To which I replied, "Adjustment is always a downward movement. The upward movement is never an adjustment—it is always a commitment."

I call upon the church to make a commitment to remodel itself until it becomes the best thing that has ever happened to the human race. The church becomes the best friend for all people when we proclaim the Gospel of Faith—Hope—and Love which truly stimulates and sustains human self-esteem.

It was in the summer of 1967 that I attended the World Psychiatric Congress in Madrid, Spain. There were over four thousand psychiatrists and psychologists (and only a few theologians) gathered from around the world. The closing plenary session was listed in the program: "Human Values in Psychotherapy." The first lecturer was Dr. H. P. Rome. He spoke for thirty minutes on "Faith." "Never undermine your patients' faith," he said. "Build on it!"

The second lecturer was Dr. H. W. Janz. He spoke for thirty minutes on "Hope." "What is hope?" he asked. "It is a phenomenon!" he answered. "Nobody knows what hope is, but we have all seen the miracles that happen in a patient when 'somehow hope enters their life.'"

The third lecturer was Dr. C. A. Seguin. He spoke on "Love." "Nonjudgmental, unconditional love is the most healing force in the world," he declared.

I was jubilant, of course! This doctrine of love is the classic doctrine of grace lifted from Christian theology!

"Faith, hope, love"—the gospel of Christ rightly perceived and proclaimed is the healing hope for every person.

May we discover its power anew. For the positive gospel is God's pathway to human dignity.

PART I

A New Reformation: The Desperate Need

Chapter One

A New Reformation: The Desperate Need

WHAT THE CHURCH NEEDS, more than anything else, is a new reformation—nothing less will do! Without a new theological reformation, the Christian church as the authentic body of Christ may not survive.

As a Christian, a theologian, and a churchman within the Reformed tradition, I must believe that it is possible for the church to exist even though it may be in serious error in substance, strategy, style, or spirit. Martin Luther faced this haunting and recurring question: "Am I alone right and is all the rest of the church wrong?"

The tradition of Luther or Calvin gives us this conviction: the church of Jesus Christ stands always in the frail, human arena of imperfection. Yet, if granted the grace of humility, the church will be equipped to go on with the unfinished tasks of reforming and refining its mission and message under the Lordship of Jesus Christ in the power of the Holy Spirit.

The sixteenth-century Reformation can today be viewed as a reactionary movement—a "mid-flight correction," to use a twentieth-century space-flight term. If the birth of the church in the first century is seen as the launching of this Vehicle of Redemptive Communication, then the

25

Protestant Reformation was, in fact, a "mid-flight correction." It is time now, at the end of the second millennium of church history, for another "mid-flight correction." Without it, this vehicle—the institutional church—will continue off course. However serious or slight that misdirection might be, the final destination will be disastrously distorted.

What indications seem evident that the church is off-course in its methodology? What symptoms reveal that it is not the healthy body of believers that it should be?

Why do I believe that the redefinition and reformation of theology is necessary?

If we ask ourselves the right questions, the need will become terribly obvious.

1. *Do you know professing believers who lack the emotional and spiritual wholeness that a healthy Christian religion should produce?*

Surely, we cannot accept as a viable, valued faith any religion that fails to produce emotionally healthier human beings. "By their fruits shall you know them," Jesus said. At the same time we must remember these words of Samuel Shoemaker, "The church is a hospital for sinners, not a museum for saints." Yet, we must face the reality that the church has far too high a percentage of its faithful adherents who remain infected with a negative self-image and a very low self-esteem.

Doubtless every pastor has felt the anguish of seeing members of his flock fail to reflect the joy and enthusiasm in living. And we wonder why. The answer, I believe, becomes clear as we recognize the fact that prayer, worship, and well-thought-out sermons will not produce morally strong and spiritually exciting Christians if they fail to produce self-confident, inwardly secure, nondefensive, integrated persons. What we need is a theology of salvation that begins and ends with a recognition of every person's hunger for glory.

2. *How do we explain, justify, and tolerate the destructive disunity and suspicions between the various sectors in Christianity?*
Divisive, suspicious tensions continue to disrupt what should be a beautiful unity of love among the followers of Christ. "Labeling" remains dangerously fashionable. Labels such as, "evangelical," "fundamental," "charismatic," "liberal" contribute to polarization and produce a climate of implied or outspoken distrust. Respectful dialogue becomes virtually impossible. What we desperately need to offset this disunity and distrust is a new and cleansing theology of communication.

3. *Are we aware that theology has failed to accommodate and apply proven insights in human behavior as revealed by twentieth-century psychologists?*
A widespread tension has too long existed between psychologists and theologians. Both disciplines should be committed to the healing of the human spirit. Both can and must learn from each other. Neither one can claim to have "the whole truth." Conflict between theology and psychology points to a need for growth and accommodation until the contradiction in thought is reconciled on the altar of truth. What we need is a theological restructuring which synergizes scientific and spiritual truth as related to the human being.

4. *Consider the failure of Protestant Christianity to come up with a dynamic movement to correct social injustices after successfully proclaiming the gospel. Can this be a result of a fundamental defect in our basic theology?*
There is a seeming irreconcilable chasm and tension between "The Gospel of Salvation" and "The Social Gospel."

The relatively rare efforts of sincere evangelical leaders to bridge the gap in order to fulfill the divine imperative to apply the gospel to the social and political injustices have failed to produce any measurable, manageable, movement. What we need now is a theology of social ethics that emerges spontaneously from a theology of salvation.

5. *How do we resolve the perceived conflict posed by advocates of a so-called "theology of comfort and success" versus a "theology of discipleship under the cross"?*

There is a great deal of confusion in the minds of individuals and the entire church body when it comes to the pursuit of personal happiness and prosperity. Are comfort and success to be denied to Christians? The church has frequently been divided unnecessarily into conflicting camps where success and comfort are seen as noble values by some and ignoble if not unchristian values by others. I believe the conflict can be resolved when the confusion is dissolved. And the confusion can and will be dissolved when we come to see that the truth is a paradox: there is no success without sacrifice. There is no comfort without costly commitment. I submit that a Theology of Self-Esteem will give rise to a Theology of Possibility Thinking and a Theology of Possibility Thinking will inspire "success through sacrificial service." In that process the confusion will be cleared up and the conflict resolved.

6. *Is it possible to reconcile the terrible tension that exists between sincere Christians who call themselves "Marxist" and equally sincere Christians who could be described as "Anti-Marxist"?*

Believers can be found who are equally sincere advocates of the "socialistic ideology" applied to the Christian faith and life, while others hold with equal passion to, for want of a better label, "capitalistic ideology." But there is far more than an economic philosophy involved here. The tension is not only the debate over the distribution of wealth. Rather, the issue goes much deeper and centers around what might be called a "Theology of Motivation Suffocation" and a "Theology of Incentive Impulse." Surely a religion that fails to inspire a noble incentive impulse in the human spirit cannot be judged as truly creative and productive and, therefore, functionally wholesome. What is needed is a positive Theology of Economics that is built around the human being's deepest needs.

7. *If the gospel of Jesus Christ is the truth that we proclaim it to be, then why is the established church in Europe and America declining, and why is the world not rushing in to accept the "Good News"?*

Mainline Protestantism continues to decline in membership in America as well as in the so-called Christian nations in Europe and Scandinavia, where a pitifully small percentage take their religion seriously. And the vital signs of the state-supported church in Western Europe are so weak that we have cause to wonder if that institutional body is not actually dead. Indeed, if state support was removed, we might discover that, in fact, the old church is dead. I believe so many churches today are missing the vital theological spark that is inherent in the core of the gospel but has not been perceived, valued adequately, or accepted. What is needed is a positive Theology of Evangelism.

8. *Can the human needs being met by spreading secularism not be fulfilled more effectively by the gospel of Christ if it is rightly interpreted and proclaimed?*

Secularism has swept across the world like a raging forest fire, consuming the culture that had its roots in Western civilization—a culture largely flowered from the faith of classical Judeo-Christianity. It seems that most every aspect of Western culture has been ravaged by the conflagration, including art, music, language, theatre, marriage, and the family. All have been shaken to their foundations in the twentieth century while a thriving, prosperous secularism laughs at the dying, institutional church and scorns her values and ways.

And while this is going on, the institutional church denominations gather for their annual synods and conventions and spend thousands of hours debating amendments to amendments and playing the game of religious institutionalism according to *Robert's Rule of Order*. In the process, they fail to articulate a singular, exciting plan to launch a successful offensive against its arch enemy—secularism. Where is the flaming faith that can be fanned to sweep the young generations who today are still in wombs and cribs and playpens? What is desperately needed is a positive and exciting theology of mission that can win the world in the next millennium.

9. How can the worldwide body of believers be motivated to fulfill the great commission and begin to care with compassion for suffering souls worldwide?

What is needed is a strong theology of mission to awaken the slumbering church to the task of world evangelization in keeping with our Lord's command. Many sincere students within the larger body of believers are turned off by a theology that offers nothing more than a classical heaven and hell proposition. The alternative theology of mission focuses on peace, brotherhood, and economic equality. And the tension between these two theologies of mission is strong in the church today. Somehow a strong fresh theology of mission must be articulated that will allow sincere followers of both points of view to merge mind, motive, method, and message.

These nine questions must be faced with brutal honesty within a despair-preventing context and solution-offering setting. For to ask such penetrating questions without the hope of solutions can only lead to despair and defeat, and to be diagnostic without offering positive prescriptions can be more dangerous than ignorance. Any diagnosis that has reason to expect negative findings must surely be made in a hope-inducing environment. In asking these questions and commenting briefly on them, I do so from a strong base of hope. I'm convinced that a dynamic theology which reflects the authentic gospel of Jesus Christ offers redeeming solutions to all of the agonizing tensions found in the nine questions.

All of the problems, pressures, and perils addressed in the preceding questions arise from a basic defect in much of modern Christianity. What is that basic flaw? I believe it is the failure to proclaim the gospel in a way that can satisfy every person's deepest need—one's spiritual hunger for glory. Rather than glorify God's highest creation— the human being—Christian liturgies, hymns, prayers, and scriptural interpretations have often insensitively and destructively offended the dignity of the person. The human ego has been labeled as the ultimate sin, when, in fact, it is the mark of the image of God within people. The ego has been understood as something that must be destroyed or annihilated, when, in reality, it is to be redeemed.

Oddly enough, in twenty centuries, the church has moved forward without understanding or acknowledging this question: *What is the deepest need of human beings?* The church has survived through these centuries by assuming that every person's ultimate need was "salvation from sin." It has held out "hope for forgiveness" as the ultimate answer.

What's wrong with this interpretation today? Nothing, and yet, everything, if in the process of interpreting sin and repentance the gospel is presented in substance or spirit in a way that assaults a person's self-esteem. Not to understand that truth, or to be casual or cavalier in responding to every person's need for dignity, will perpetuate the problems offered in the previous questions.

Meanwhile in the twentieth century, nineteen centuries after the birth of Jesus Christ, an academically disciplined profession, psychiatry, has dared to ask the all-important question: What is the ultimate nature and will of the human being? Pitifully, theologians have abandoned an essentially theological question to other disciplines and professions.

Although he did not question, "What is the ultimate nature of and will of the human being?" Karl Marx, who dealt with the obvious, material things, seemed to respond when he proposed a view of the human being as a materialistic creature. And the Marxist diagnosis for the human being's deepest needs was "Economic Equality." Hence, he offered a materialistic solution as the panacea for jealousy, war, and strife—peace through economic revolution.

What is wrong with this diagnosis and prescription? The answer is found in the fact that the needs of persons are far deeper than the economist would suggest. The human being is a spiritual creature whose deepest needs can only be met and satisfied on a spiritual level. So Marx missed the mark!

Sigmund Freud, following Marx closely on the calendar, probed deeper. "The human being's deepest need is pleasure" became the irreducible ideological building block of Freudian psychology. Under Freud the "will to pleasure" became the hub of the philosophical system that seeks to understand the human being's irreducible need. It is no surprise that good Freudians seldom made good Marxists because at the deepest level the contradictions in the doctrine of the human being make them virtually irreconcilable.

Not the "will to pleasure," but the "will to power" would be Alfred Adler's analysis of the deepest human need. It was easy under his philosophical umbrella to see the short-sightedness of the Freudian position. Men have too often been driven with such a lust for power that they have sacrificed their women, their sex lives, and their Freudian pleasures on the altar of an all-consuming passion for power.

If the "will to pleasure" was the Freudian analysis, and the "will to power" was Adler's analysis, then the "will to meaning" could sum up the position of Viktor Frankl. An essential spirituality inevitably permeates the positive posture of this late twentieth century founder of "logotherapy." Not a few theologians have found his analysis of the human being to be compatible with sacred Scripture.

The time has come now, nearly 500 years since the Protestant Reformation, for theologians and Christians in general to pass judgment on the answers given by these men to what is the ultimate theological question. For the crisis facing the church now is a crisis of theology that centers on the doctrine of the human being.

The single most important question facing the world today is: What is this creature called the human being? We have, very briefly, examined the positions of Karl Marx, Sigmund Freud, Alfred Adler, and Viktor Frankl concerning their view of persons and their needs. It is now time for us to look at the answer offered by Jesus Christ. And that answer must then become the primary value by which we judge our theological position. For the universal church can only survive the revolutionary future if it meets the deepest, classical—not fashionable—needs of every living person.

In my earlier book, *Self-Love: The Dynamic Force of Success,* I first presented my case: The "will to self-love" is the deepest of all human desires. Because the human being is created in the image of God, the will to dignity is the irreducible, psychological, and spiritual nucleus around which the life of the human soul revolves and evolves. The need for dignity, self-worth, self-respect, and self-esteem is the deepest of all human needs.

If our need for dignity is assaulted or ignored by the church, then truly we are "lost sinners." Unsaved and unfulfilled, we will be naturally led down a destructive road of ego-tripping. Unsatisfied, we will be restless, bored, and drawn to launch dangerous adventures—wars included. Unsatiated, our hunger for pride as a prince or princess of heaven will drive us to destructive power and dishonest manipulations. An immense, complex tangle of negative emotions will be woven around our poor lost souls.

The "will to pleasure" is not in error; it is simply shallow. For the frenetic attempt by hedonistic creatures to madly pursue amoral pleasures is really a fearful attempt of non-self-respecting persons to escape the threatening possibility of frightfully facing and seeing themselves as persons most difficult to accept and love.

What is really the driving force behind the hedonism and the immorality in the human race? It is precisely every person's need for self-respect. Tragically, we don't value ourselves highly enough to dare to trust positive relationships—both human and divine relationships that could generate the secure and satisfying stimulations that would cause us to be emotionally immune to hedonistic pleasures. So, non-self-esteeming human beings, fearful of commitments to valued relationships, are driven in personal panic still further into the desert of despair, hoping to escape the anguish of seeing themselves as they are. They must escape loneliness; solitude could be too embarrassing.

The "will to power" can be understood as an outgrowth of our deeper need for self-worth. It is not really power, but it's pride that drives us all. "If I achieve power, I'll be famous. People will respect me, and I'll be proud of who I am." Thus the non-analyzed, non-articulated subconscious rationale operates. The power-path is ultimately unfulfilling. The "will to power" leads to a dangerous ego trip. It is dangerous and ultimately unfulfilling because it focuses on the self instead of others. The self-esteem trip, by contrast, satisfies a person's ego needs by finding fulfillment in the service to Christ and others.

Even the "will to meaning" is meaningless until it is seen in the perspective of a deeper need—self-dignity, self-worth, self-respect, and self-esteem. With meaning, my human life retains dignity; without it, I lose all hope of self-esteem.

No theological question is more important than this: "What is the human being that you care about him? or the children of human beings that you care about them?" (Heb. 2:6, translation mine). It is the question that finds its answer first in the Creation, and finally in the Incarnation, the Crucifixion, and the Resurrection of Jesus Christ. No theology will long last nor will it ever succeed unless it begins with and keeps its focus on satisfying every person's hunger for personal value.

All of the problems facing the church will find healing answers if we start with and do not get distracted at any time from meeting every person's deepest need—his hunger for self-esteem, self-worth, and personal dignity. This means that human dignity becomes the ultimate human value. It is the indivisible cell, the nonnegotiable need, the uncompromising quality of humanity. When persons lose their dignity, they lose their humanity. A person can survive without power and pleasure, but he cannot survive if he loses all pride in being a person! So the self-esteem of every human soul must become the healthy core of our humanity-helping religion.

The problems facing the church have arisen in part because religious leaders, teachers, theologians, evangelists, social reformers, and critics have not been able to communicate creatively and constructively. They are all coming from different points, positions, and postures; consequently they are doomed to disunity.

Historical theology has dictated and directed that the starting point for many theologians and Christian leaders will be the Scriptures. That sounds sensational. Who would challenge that? Yet history shows that, as a starting point, disagreement over interpretations of Scripture lead to divisiveness. For instance, advocates of biblical inerrancy are themselves disagreed on issues such as premillennialism; infant baptism vs. adult immersion, etc.

Other classical systematic theologians would begin with the doctrine of God. But this is part of the reason the church is in the predicament it is in today. The problems facing the church will never be respectfully discussed and constructively dealt with by starting from this theological position. In fact, in many religious circles, there are suspicions about the faith, doctrine, and theology of religious leaders outside their own particular circle. We can never communicate until we establish a fresh starting point that transcends historical theological differences.

Wayne Alderson was the vice president of operations at Pittron Steel Foundry in Glassport, Pennsylvania. The plant was agonizing under the crunch of racial dissension, labor tensions, and management anxieties. "Could the Christian faith apply values to bring healing and productivity to a strife-torn plant?" Wayne wondered. For eighty-four days the strike went on at Pittron. The leader of the United Steel Workers of America union in that area was a man named Sam Piccolo.

"Sam Piccolo hated me," Wayne admits. "And if the truth were known, I didn't think too much of him either. But he had to establish some sensible foundation on which we could agree."

Alderson, a strong fundamental Christian, recounts the scene. "We couldn't agree on the Bible. We couldn't agree on Jesus. We couldn't agree on theology. What we did agree on was the need for the individual man and woman to be valued." Based on the dignity of the person, Wayne lived out what I call a Christian theology of self-esteem—visiting people in their homes, going to the hospital to see them, etc. "That tough union president began to see I was really concerned about his people," Wayne reports. "He said to me, 'Wayne, what I am beginning to see is that you love people. You care about my people!' At that point," Alderson says, "he started to value me."[1]

As a result of that dignity-producing reconciliation approach, the strike was finally settled. Bible study groups formed in the factory. "Operation Turnaround" was launched successfully. Productivity soared. The company value skyrocketed! And Wayne Alderson is traveling around the world with his ministry beautifully titled, "Value of the Person."

I suggest that sincere Christians and church-persons can find a theological launching point of universal agreement if they can agree on the universal right and uncompromising need of every person to be treated with great respect simply because he or she is a human being!

The "Dignity of the Person" will then be the new theological bench mark! Is there not a strong possibility that most sincere Christians might agree on this as the starting point, the undebatable standard, the human ideal? I offer theology of self-esteem as a starting position which will hopefully generate a climate and control for respectful discussion and constructive response to the challenges faced by the church today.

One day I noticed my gardener was wearing two watches, one on the right arm and the other on the left. "Why," I asked, "are you wearing two watches?" "Oh, I wear this watch to check up on that watch," he answered. "But how can you be sure which watch is right and which is wrong?" I asked.

I went on to tell him about Greenwich mean time, the international universal time standard. By it, all clocks are ultimately set. "Can you imagine," I told him, "what would happen if suddenly Moscow insisted that their central clock was standard? Then London would protest and say that Big Ben was the irreducible right time, and America would probably go by the wrist watch of the President of the United States." Without a standard there would be international pandemonium. The world must agree on one single, nondebatable fixed reference point for time-keeping.

In similar fashion ships at sea in the northern hemisphere have their nondebatable point of reference, the North Star. And musicians worldwide always come back to concert "A" as their agreed upon standard. Concert "A" is always "440" vibrations per second. Can you imagine the disharmony in music if there were no international standard?

Theologians must have their international, universal, transcreedal, transcultural, transracial standard. It could be the inviolable, inherited right of every human being to be offered the opportunity to enjoy self-dignity—the sacred legacy—the pride of being a member of God's human race.

Yes, what we need in the worldwide Christian church today is nothing less than a new reformation. Where the sixteenth-century Reformation returned our focus to sacred Scriptures as the only infallible rule for faith and practice, the new reformation will return our focus to the sacred right of every person to self-esteem! The fact is, the church will never succeed until it satisfies the human being's hunger for self-value.

Now, if we agree that the church is the divine vehicle of redemptive communication, and that a "mid-flight correction" is necessary, the dignity of the human being is the "North Star" of our voyage, then where can we go for a more detailed guideline to chart our potentially dangerous course?

Somehow in our sincere effort to reform our church

theology today, we must avoid the destructive and divisive results that occurred within the church in the sixteenth century. Where the Protestant Reformation was a reactionary movement, the twentieth-century Reformation must be a reconciling movement. Luther and Calvin, we know, looked to the Book of Romans in the Bible for their primary inspiration. Were they, unknowingly, possessed more by the spirit of St. Paul than by the Spirit of Jesus Christ? Are we not on safer grounds if we look to our Lord's words to launch our reformation?

I propose that we begin with our Lord's Prayer. More than anything else, it holds the hopeful prospect of becoming the universally agreeable starting point by which a new reformation can begin. It can serve as the instrument panel by which the "mid-flight correction" of the Vehicle of Redemptive Communication can be responsibly and positively made. Here Christians may discover a positive power in a theology that is centered on Christ—the Ideal One, the Ultimate Person, the Universal Human Standard. For the Lord's Prayer points us to the Person, the power, and the pathway to real self-dignity. As we focus on Jesus Christ, we shall discover a new theology, one that offers salvation from shame to self-esteem. We shall discover that self-esteem rooted in Christ's love finally satisfies every person's thirst for glory.

And the result will be a faith that will bring glory to the human race for the greater glory of God.

The prospects will be a message that promises success to the church. And that's good news, for the alternative is failure. Only non-Christians or anti-Christians should advocate failure to Christ's movement.

The glorious hope will be a society of civility where people really treat each other beautifully! And the end result will be transformed and redeemed persons. Persons inwardly secure enough to live open, transparent, and honest lives. Healthy persons who will really feel good about themselves because their ego needs are met in sincere services, rather than in stuffy status. And God will be glorified by the personalities and performance of these human beings who are called "His Children."

Where shall we begin?

Join me at the feet of our Lord.

Let us pray.

"Our Father. . . ."

PART II

The Lord's Prayer: His Healing Way

Chapter Two

The Lordship of Christ

WHY DO I SUGGEST that the Lord's Prayer is the instrument panel which can serve the church and the private Christian in making the necessary mid-flight correction?

To begin with, the Lord's Prayer is a call to humility. We cannot experience renewal within the church until we are humble enough to admit failure, acknowledge fallibility, and declare our need to change and grow.

The need for a positive, intellectual humility among religious leaders of the major faiths is paramount. Too many Bible teachers, lay ministers, ordained clergy, theological professors, and religious editors operate from the assumption that they have graduated. They do not see their role as continuing students, but, rather as "professors" who have arrived and whose only mission is to indoctrinate others. We must all see ourselves as persons in the process of growth who still have areas in our own lives where growth could and should occur. We are insecure and irresponsible so long as we cannot and dare not admit that we might be perpetuating errors of interpretation; we might be imperfect in our judgment of our positions; and there are still some areas of our intelligence that are not fully enlightened.

43

Only deeply secure people with a strong, positive self-image dare to admit that they too need to grow and change. Only the person with a healthy self-esteem dares to admit "I'm not perfect. I need to make changes somewhere in my system." By contrast inwardly insecure persons do not dare to ask dangerous questions which threaten their own well-established traditional positions. This may explain why it is difficult for some people who have reached professional prominence to admit, "I was wrong." "I still have much to learn." "I have my own blind spots." "I have areas in my own thought system where I need to grow." "I am more interested in being right than in being applauded by my peers, my students, my colleagues, my supporters, and my cohorts."

Only the humble dare to ask questions. Arrogance has no time for the sincere interrogative approach; it only has time for pronouncements. No wonder the nonquestioning approach and the autocratic or hierarchical mentality stifles dialogue and sets the tone for demagoguery and the breakdown of human relations. There will be no renewal in the church without humility.

The Lord's Prayer will serve us well as it illuminates the first quality we will need for growth. The Lord's Prayer will be the inspiration for genuine humility, and it will lead us to accept the Lordship of Christ.

Assuming that the church achieves positive humility, admits error, and confesses to failure, then where do we go? What, or who, will remake, renew, and reform us? What supreme authority will be the architect of our theological reconstruction?

We cannot simply anoint self-esteem as our philosophical supreme authority unless it is in fact the centrifugal force in the mind and heart of Christ. If it is merely a humanly contrived apologetic, it cannot stand as a philosophical authority, for self-esteem will not be without its own unique contradictions. Christ must be Lord over the ultimate human value. Any theological suggestion that self-esteem is to be the bench mark of our theology loses integrity, authenticity, and must be branded as counterfeit and contrived secular humanism unless it is central to the concern of Christ.

Shall we be satisfied with the traditional and predictable Protestant position? The sacred Scriptures are our infallible rule for faith and practice. And we have insisted that in and through the Bible, God's eternal truth is communicated.

But can anything be above the Scriptures? Yes, the Eternal Word transcends the written Word. Christ is the Word made flesh. Christ is the Lord over the Scriptures; the Scriptures are not Lord over Christ.

The inspiration of sacred Scriptures has been under attack and has understandably produced a reaction that would have us believe that the most crucial issue facing Christendom is biblical inerrancy. Serious as this may be, it must not detract us from a higher, holier, healthier issue: the Lordship of Jesus Christ.

For unless Christ through his Holy Spirit controls the believers in him and in his Word, we shall continue to see his followers remain dangerously divided over biblical interpretation. So, Christ must be accepted as Lord over the Scriptures. The Bible must not compete with the Lord for the seat of glory. We are "saved by the blood," not "by the Book." We believe in the holy Trinity, not a holy Quadrangle.

For when an apparent contradiction or conflict or confusion exists within the sacred Scriptures, how shall the argument be settled? What interpretation shall reign? Whose opinion shall stand? And what will happen when self-esteem theologians have their own sincere and serious differences? Then let Christ enter our minds as Lord over all.

The answers will be found in Jesus Christ, our Savior

and Lord. Before his feet we bow, and in his Spirit we prayerfully and humbly seek a resolution.

If we can agree on the need to bend our theological thinking to the Lordship of Christ, then we must ask this question: "What is our Lord's deepest desire?" What is his highest hope, most pressing passion, and crucial concern? If Jesus Christ could stand before you and me and before your Christian church and mine, how would he complete this sentence: "But the real issue is. . . ."?

If we can agree that a Christian is to be an extension of the life of Christ in the world, and that the church is to be the body of Christ, then should not our first order of business be to search out the mind and will of our Lord for his followers today? Can we not all see the temptation to allow other political, commercial, and institutional concerns to take priority in our daily lives? And if we succumb to this temptation, is it not logical to expect that we might be misguided in our Christian work and witness?

Can we not honestly hope that if the church as a body and Christian persons as individual believers give first priority to discovering the central concern in the mind of Christ, that then and only then might the church hope to fulfill its divine purpose?

I submit that we will find our response to these questions as we probe for the answer to another vital question: "What, oh Lord Jesus Christ, is your deepest concern for me as a person and for your church as an institution today?" And, having asked this dangerous question, how can we expect to discover our Lord's answer?

A simple and very wise man once said: "If you really want to know a person's deepest desire and most conscientious concern, study, if you can, his unvarnished prayers. Stealthily approach him in his intimate closet and try to overhear what he is really praying about passionately."

If we are then courageous, humble, and sincere enough to discover our Lord's imperative for his followers today, we can hardly go wrong by studying the prayer that Christ gave to his disciples and to us with the suggestion that we pray daily. Surely, we can expect Christ's divine directive to be contained within the substance of the prayer that he gave us. I suggest then that we can discover that Christ will reveal his deepest concern for you, for me, and for all believers today if we will study the prayer that down through the centuries has been called "The Lord's Prayer."

What is our Lord's greatest passion for his church today? I believe that he wants his followers to respect themselves as equal children of God and to treat all other human beings with that same respect.

"Our Father" is a call to be a family, and it is an invitation to find our pride in belonging to God's family. So, what would Jesus say if he could speak to us today? Would he tell us what miserable sinners we are? I think not.

Deep down in our hearts I believe we know that Jesus would say something like this to us: "You are the salt of the earth. You are the light of the world. You are a child of the Eternal. Follow me and I will make you fishers of men.

"Receive and enjoy the fruit of salvation: Self-esteem, self-worth. Hear God's call to you. He would save you for high and holy service—to be proud of who you are. Then, stop putting yourself down. Start enjoying the dignity that is your God-intended destiny."

If the gospel of Jesus Christ can be proclaimed as a theology of self-esteem, imagine the health this could generate in society! Consider the immeasurable, myriad mixtures of human tragedies resulting from persons and institutions consumed by their "ego" problems. Now imagine how society can be prevented from these perils if human beings find their ego fulfillment and their heart's hunger for glory fully satisfied in a beautiful relationship with Christ and his family.

Chapter Three

Liberated
to Love

NOW, LET THE LORD'S Prayer in our life bring the Lordship of Christ over our life.

Since our self-esteem—high or low—will affect every area of our life, it is imperative that it come under the control of Christ. Everything we do and are will be a reflection of our self-image, positive or negative. Until Christ controls our self-image, he is not in fact Lord over our life.

Surely Christ never puts down a human being, "For God sent the Son into the world, not to condemn . . ." (John 3:17). He builds up, redeems, and sanctifies persons and personalities. We might even conclude—at least have reason to suspect—that the level of the Lordship of Christ in a life can be measured by the rising level of Christian self-worth.

And so we ask: how can the Lord's Prayer lift us from shame to self-esteem?

The Lord's Prayer clears the way for a healthy theology of self-esteem, for it deals with the classic negative emotions that destroy our self-dignity. The Lord's Prayer offers Christ's positive solution from these six basic, negative emotions that infect and affect our self-worth:

1) Inferiority: "Our Father who art in heaven,
   Hallowed be thy name."
2) Depression: "Thy kingdom come, Thy will be done,
   On earth as it is in heaven."
3) Anxiety: "Give us this day our daily bread;"
4) Guilt: "And forgive us our debts,"
5) Resentment: "As we also have forgiven our debtors;"
6) Fear: "And lead us not into temptation,
   But deliver us from evil."

1. *Inferiority,* the primary negative emotion that blocks our self-esteem, is dealt with when we are reminded that God is our Father. His name is *honorable.* The human race was designed to be his family. Then every human being has potential value. Every person has undeveloped possibilities.

2. *Depression.* Now the Lord's Prayer moves on to replace this negative emotion with healing hope. *"Thy kingdom come, thy will be done."* That's another way of saying that God has a kingdom, a plan, a dream, which can include any and every person. All persons are offered the possibility of honorable service. Such being the case, no person is too small for God's love and no service is too insignificant for God's honor. As we experience liberation from shame to a noble self-love, we are inspired to dream the kind of dreams that generate self-esteem which motivates us to serve our God and our fellow family members.

3. *Anxiety,* the third self-esteem-destroying emotion, is replaced by silent security through the words, *"Give us this day our daily bread."*

What if God gives me a noble dream, a high calling, and *I find I don't have what it takes?* Will I succeed or fail? Is success important? Yes, it is terribly important. For nothing is more destructive to a person's self-esteem than the fear of being a terrible failure! If the church genuinely cares about a person's total life, we will do all we can to lead and lift every person into self-affirming experiences. Self-affirmation is success. God, who deals with our inferiority, will handle our anxiety over success and failure, too.

4. *Guilt* is the next negative emotion that is sure to pollute one's self-respect. Sincere, self-affirmed, divine-adventurers, striving to succeed, will be tempted to perfectionism which is not realistic and will generate genuine guilt. The Lord's Prayer does not encourage us to abandon noble missions for fear we cannot do a perfect job. Rather, we are encouraged to accept forgiveness while we continue uncompromisingly to pursue excellence. So, the problem of guilt will be real.

"Why didn't I do it this way?" is a negative emotion that will be encountered by any sincere Christian who finds God's dream and pursues it, or neglects it.

"Why didn't I do a better job with the dreams God gave me? Why didn't I take better advantage of his wonderful opportunities?" Self-condemnation, self-flagellation, regrets, and guilts will pile up too fast in the sincere Christian mind. How opportune then is the spacing of this phrase, *"Forgive us our trespasses [debts]."*

5. *Resentment.* Even as we experience the Lord's forgiving grace when we experience his acceptance of us as imperfect persons, we are now called to accept ourselves, too, as imperfect persons. Then we must move on to transfer this divine grace by accepting others with their imperfections. In doing so, we will be saved from the negative emotions of resentment. Welcome now this healing petition: "Forgive me my trespasses *as I forgive those who trespass against me.*" As we pray these words, our evolving self-esteem will be protected with the invisible shield of gracious forgiveness which immunizes us from resentment.

6. *Fear.* What remains to complete the cycle of growing self-esteem? It is immunization against that final negative emotion, fear, which, if left to attack the self-affirming

soul, could destroy the courage to love, and the whole self-esteem system would unravel because fear makes love impossible. And there can be no self-respect without love. "The greatest . . . is love" (1 Cor. 13:13).

Dr. Gerald Jampolsky, a prominent American psychiatrist and head of the Center for Attitudinal Healing in Tiburon, California, who lectures before audiences from the American Psychiatric Association to television talk shows has been preaching this theme: "The two basic emotions are not love and hate, but love and fear." The opposite of love is not hate, but fear. What is fear but the absence of love? And what is the absence of love but the presence of fear?

"Lead us not into temptation, but deliver us from evil." This is the strong summary sentence that sustains our maturing self-esteem by dealing a death blow to real fear . . . making authentic love really possible.

So in one masterful, classical little paragraph, "The Lord's Prayer," we have a therapeutic spiritual exercise that replaces the self-esteem-strangulating, negative emotions with positive, health-generating emotions!

Truly, the Lord's prayer in our life will bring the Lordship of Christ over our life. Wholeness, salvation, and healing will be experienced and will touch every aspect of our lives!

Let us look now at how this healing path unfolds.

Chapter Four

The Fatherhood of God

THE STARTING POINT to building a solid self-esteem must be a reconciliation of the estranged Father-child relationship.

Two universal human qualities must here be noted. The first is a universal "ego" problem in the human being. I believe that this ego drive is the frustrated hunger for glory that haunts the human being who misses the wholesome fulfillment of this need for pride—a healthy fulfillment that would be realized were he reconciled to the glorious side of our heavenly Father. With perceptive insight Bishop Fulton J. Sheen, outstanding Christian and popular television personality of a generation ago, wrote, "the egoist is one who cannot bring himself to cooperate or communicate with others; all his anxieties are those of sustaining his own ego, not those of striving for perfection." Destructive pride, or an ego-problem, stems from the fact that we were created to be princes and princesses, sharing the creative glory with the heavenly Father. Alienation spoiled all of that. When we are reconciled with the Father, a healthy, humble pride comes over us. We are at peace. But until then we are restless.

As St. Augustine said, "Our souls are restless till they

52

rest in Thee." This explains the second human quality we should now note. It is the universal religious "instinct" within the human being. For example, even though she was raised in an atheistic home and society, the daughter of Joseph Stalin found the spiritual impulses strong and irresistible. And a parallel to this is also seen in the life of the salmon as it is directed mysteriously to its origin in a remote river tributary. As human beings, there is a marvelous, mysterious, spiritual magnetic pull that tugs on the human heart.

A member of our church, Mary Nelson, had tried for years without success to interest her hairdresser Vivian in attending our church. Again and again Vivian made it clear that she and her husband, Herb, weren't interested. She was also critical of the money spent to erect the massive buildings which comprise the church complex, including the Crystal Cathedral and the fourteen-story Tower of Hope with its ninety-foot cross.

Then the miracle happened. Mary tells it like this.

"Last Monday, September 21, 1981, I called Vivian to make a hair appointment for the following day. When she answered the telephone and I told her who was calling, she said, 'Mary, I was almost ready to call you.' Then Vivian went on to tell me that she had been very upset because of what had happened to Herb the week before.

"It seems that on Saturday evening Herb and Vivian had gone to the baseball game at Anaheim Stadium. While they were watching the game, Herb said, 'I've got to get out of here for awhile. The people behind us are smoking and it is getting to me.' Herb went to the lower level for some fresh air.

"After a half hour or so Vivian became worried when Herb didn't return, so she went out to look for him. Vivian didn't find Herb where she had expected him to be. With growing feelings of worry and concern, she continued her search until she heard a voice behind her asking, 'Are you looking for me?'

"Vivian told him that she had begun to worry about him

when he hadn't come back to their seats. And Herb said, 'Vivian, you don't need to worry about me anymore.'

"When Vivian asked him what he meant, he told her that he had been standing where he could look across to 'Mary's church.' And he went on to describe his feelings as he looked at the lighted cross and the light reflections on the Crystal Cathedral. All of this turned his thoughts to God, and then Herb said, 'Vivian, I have made my peace with God, let's go home now.'

"Vivian and Herb walked out together to a point where they could see the Crystal Cathedral with its towering cross. While standing there, Vivian had a strange feeling. 'It was as if God were present at that very moment,' she said. Vivian and Herb then left the stadium for home. As they were driving on the freeway, Herb began to fight for breath, and he said to Vivian, who was driving, 'I hope I can make it home.' However, Herb got worse, so Vivian decided that she had better get off of the freeway for some help.

"Vivian told me that she just picked a nearby off-ramp and ended up in a residential area. She then stopped the car and went to three doors before she could get someone to respond. At the third house the lady who answered the door realized there was a serious problem and called the paramedics. She then asked Vivian, 'I'm a Christian, what can I do to help?' The lady then ran out to the car where she found Herb leaning against it and gasping for air. She immediately began to pray, but Herb slumped to the ground and died before the paramedics could arrive."

How do we explain the attraction to God by persons who claim to be "irreligious"?

The answer may be found in the fact that the Fatherhood of God is built into our subconsciousness. And until we experience a reconciliation with God, we are victims of an inferiority complex that inevitably follows extrications from our natural roots. For this reason the Lord's Prayer begins with a call to family reconciliation—the initial step to eliminating the first obstacle to self-esteem.

Recently, I received the following letter from Dorothy Carpenter who for many years has been a member of our church.

"I am writing to tell you of an incident that occurred one Sunday morning in church. I had arrived early so I could get a seat right up front below the pulpit. It wasn't long before I was aware of a conversation going on behind me.

"It was between two women—one quite young and the other a bit older. I didn't pay close attention until I heard the younger one say that sometimes she was impulsive. She then went on to say that about three months before she and a friend had gone shopping in Hollywood and became so disgusted with the high prices that they decided to go to Hong Kong to shop.

"That really got my attention. I thought if she could afford to go to Hong Kong to shop, she could surely afford Hollywood. Much to my amazement I heard her tell the other woman that she and her friend jumped on a plane, went to Hong Kong, and had a good time shopping.

"While I didn't hear it, the older lady evidently was as amazed as I, because then the truth came out. It seemed that she worked in the Los Angeles office of the Flying Tiger Airlines, and they were able to make the trip on passes.

"Now this explains where I got involved. Thirty-two years ago my son had married, and after two daughters and two years of marriage, his wife left him. I, as a grandmother, tried to stay in communication with the children and would send birthday and Christmas presents. But as time passed, I lost track of them.

"About ten years ago my daughter in Vista, California, learned through a friend that the youngest daughter of my son's first marriage lived about five miles from her. Through an interesting turn of events we made arrangements for her to have dinner with me and my present daughter-in-law and her four children. We had a wonderful time together, and in the course of our conversation she told me that her older sister had a wonderful job with the Flying Tiger Airlines.

"When I heard the young woman behind me mention the name of that line, my ears really perked up. I turned around and spoke to the young woman, 'I overheard you say that you work for the Flying Tiger Airline. I have a granddaughter whom I haven't seen for twenty-seven years who works for that airline. I don't remember her first name, but she has a younger sister named Timmy. Would you happen to know a girl with a sister named Timmy?'

"Her eyes opened wide in amazement as she said, 'I have a sister named Timmy.' In utter amazement I said, 'Could you be. . . ?' And she filled in the blank by answering, 'Maureen.'

"'That means I'm your grandmother.' With that, we both jumped up and hugged each other—much to the amazement of everyone near us.

"Dr. Schuller, she came to my home for dinner last Sunday, and I learned that Maureen has had quite a rough life, but she is a lovely thirty-one-year-old woman. I was also delighted to learn that she had an astounding spiritual experience last Christmas Eve when you invited people to come forward and accept Christ. From that time on her life has changed miraculously, and she is excited over the fact that we both are Christians and belong to the same church.

"Maureen's pilgrimage from unbeliever to the point of decision is most interesting. It seems that for seven years she had been consulting with a Christian psychiatrist who had gently been trying to point her toward a spiritual experience. Outwardly, Maureen resisted his efforts and even claimed that she hated God. But then one day not long before Christmas she happened to see and hear you on Channel 40, and she was immediately attracted to you and what you had to say.

"On Christmas Eve she felt a compulsion to go to church so she decided to attend Garden Grove Community Church. When you gave the altar call that night, she was determined not to move out of her seat. But she told me that an irresistible force seemed to move her out and down the aisle toward the front where she knelt at the altar. Christ met her there, and since then her life has been completely changed.

"Dr. Schuller, this just had to be a miracle. It's a miracle that my granddaughter and I were just a row apart on that Sunday morning when I overheard her mention the words, 'Flying Tigers.'"

Update! Maureen found mental and emotional health in reconciliation with God as her heavenly Father, and with her grandmother. Then her transformed self-image motivated her to apply for a full-time position in our church, and today she is a trusted and treasured full-time employee.

"Our Father in heaven, hallowed be your name." In this one masterful sentence our humility is assured even while our honor is established. And if my pride as a person is rooted in my relationship as a son of the Almighty, then my pride is purged of arrogance and takes the noble face of self-dignity and honor!

A neurotic fear of pride has motivated the church too long to assume the dangerous role that only Christ can safely fulfill. It is the role of keeping God's children humble without doing them more harm than good in the process. Historically, the church does not have a commendable success record in its efforts to purge sinful pride out of Christ's followers without insulting, demeaning, and bringing dishonor to God's beautiful children. In my lectures to thousands of ordained clergy of the widest cross section of historic Christianity, I have found it necessary to tell my colleagues, "Dare to be a possibility thinker! Do not fear pride; the easiest job God has is to humble us. God's almost impossible task is to keep us believing every hour of every day how great we are as his sons and daughters on planet earth.

"We need not worry about humanizing religion. Rather, we should be concerned about the greater danger—that Christianity will lose its humanity."

A high sense of self-worth based on the Fatherhood of God gives us the deep foundation for a faith and a philosophy that can build hope for human dignity! In his marvelous book entitled *Sources of Renewal*, Cardinal Karol Wojtyla, now Pope John Paul II quotes an early church father, "The living man is the Creator's glory."

What is the central, underlying theme in the Lord's Prayer? It is the priceless value of every person. The church must make this message crystal clear. We must proclaim the Good News! God wants to reclaim and redeem lost humanity. We must tell people everywhere that God wants all of us to feel good about ourselves!

Our primal problem, though, is lack of trust, *first* in oneself. Then, this lack of trust is projected onto others, God included. This is why the Lord's Prayer opens by positively attacking every person's primeval predicament—lack of trust.

Jesus begins the prayer by giving us an in-depth therapy for our inferiority complex. A human being's normal tendency is to put himself down. The Lord's Prayer deals with this at the outset. "Our Father in heaven." God is our Father. And we are his children. We are members of his family. We have God's honorable name, and that should correct our feelings of inferiority once and for all.

Consider the pride of a great family name. "If I carried one of the great family names of history and had that identification and connection, I'd really know I am somebody and I would have a strong, positive self-image," we say. But the Good News of the gospel is that we can be identified with the family of God. God can be our Father, the church can be our mother, and every other human being on planet earth that shares the faith can be our brother and sister. The Lord's Prayer calls us to this affirmation: "God is my Father! I am his child. I am somebody! I bear his honorable name."

Every psychiatrist, psychologist, sociologist, or counselor dealing in one of the healing professions that tackles the emotional problems of humanity knows that the deepest and deadliest of human emotions are anxiety, guilt, fear, and resentment. Trying to heal anybody of those negative emotions is futile until a person has developed a basic, positive self-image. And because self-esteem is foundational, inferiority complexes are the first problems that have to be corrected.

I know many Southern Californians who seem to forget the importance of a foundation when it comes to buying a house. Some of the first questions they ask are, "What kind of a view does it have?" "What is the architectural style?" "Does it have a shake roof?" "Are there any schools nearby?" "What is the resale value?" But they ignore the most important questions, "Is the ground solid?" "Will the house stand?" So there are tragedies every year when the earth gives way and expensive homes crumble because the most important factor was missing—a solid foundation.

If we have a problem in our life today, if something is missing emotionally, if there is something lacking deep in our soul, let us begin by asking ourselves the most basic question: "Do I have a positive sense of self-respect or self-esteem?" This is an important question because if there can be one generalized description of the human predicament in the world today, it would be the lack of self-esteem in human beings. Until we are conscious of our belonging to the family of God we will experience an identity crisis which will create a self-esteem crisis.

An old Norwegian tale tells it well. A boy in the woods found an egg in a nest, took it home, placed it with the eggs under a goose, and it hatched out—a freakish creature! Its deformed feet—unwebbed, clawlike—made it stumble as it tried to follow the little geese. And his beak was not flat; it was pointed and twisted. Instead of having lovely cream-colored down, it was an ugly brown color. And to top it off, he made a terrible squawking sound! He seemed to be a genetic freak—so ugly and disfigured.

Then one day a giant eagle flew across the barnyard. The eagle swept lower and lower until the strange, awkward little bird on the ground lifted his head and pointed his crooked beak into the sky. The misfit creature then stretched his wings out and began to hobble across the yard. He flapped his wings harder and harder until the wind picked him up and carried him higher and higher. He began to soar through the clouds. He had discovered what he was—he was born an eagle! And he had been trying to live like a goose.

We were born to soar. We are children of God. The tragedy is that too many human beings have never discovered their divine heritage, so they live like animals. "Our Father in heaven, honorable is your name." The Fatherhood of God offers a deep spiritual cure for the inferiority complex and lays the firm foundation for a solid spiritual self-esteem.

There are many studies today which document the scientific fact that a lack of self-esteem is at the root of alcoholism, drug addiction, teenage rebellion, marriage and family breakup, and all sorts and varieties of crime. This is why no theology of social ethics can be effective unless it starts with a theology of self-esteem that is grounded on the Fatherhood of God.

A story—historical? mythological?—vividly illustrates the point. It was during the days of the French Revolution that King Louis XVI and his queen were condemned to death. They were escorted to the guillotine in a public square in Paris and were beheaded. Then the frenzied mob called for the *dauphin:* "Bring out the prince," they cried. "He's next."

The young boy was terrified. The prince was only six years old, but he was in line to become the next king, so he had to be eliminated.

According to the storytellers, the young prince stood on the platform trembling in his black velvet coat and patent leather shoes. Long golden curls tumbled down over his shoulders. The mob screamed, "Down with royalty!" "Eliminate all royalty!" "Kill the prince!"

Suddenly a shout came out of the crowd, "Don't kill him. You'll only send his soul to heaven. That's too good for royalty. I say, turn him over to Meg, the old witch. She'll teach him filthy words. She'll teach him to be a sinner. And then, when he dies his soul will go to hell! That's what royalty deserves."

So according to the legend that's exactly what happened. The officials turned the young prince over to old Meg. The vile woman of the back alleys began to teach him dirty words. But every time the wicked woman prompted the prince to be profane he would stubbornly stamp his little feet and clench his fists, declaring, "I will not say it. I will not say those dirty words. I was born to be a king, and I won't talk that way!"

One reason many Christians have behaved so badly in the past two thousand years is because we have been taught from infancy to adulthood "how sinful" and "how worthless" we are. The self-image will always incarnate itself in action. A negative diagnosis will become a self-fulfilling prophecy. The most difficult task for the church to learn is how to deal honestly with the subject of "negativity," "sin," and "evil" without doing the cause of redemption more harm than good.

When we know that we are born to be children of God, we will be inspired to choose the noble path. When we have a tremendous sense of self-respect, we don't stoop to crime. It's beneath our dignity. When we have a consciousness that we belong to the family of God, we develop the healing, helpful, and divine sense of righteous pride. It will not be a sinful pride; it will be a redemptive pride.

So the church has some challenging questions for the secular person today. "Do you have an inner stirring— what psychologists call an existential loneliness or an internal vacuum or a hollowness inside? Is it boredom (lack of stimulation)? Is it a vague anxiety (lack of security)? Is it a nameless tension (lack of serenity)? Is it lack of self-esteem?" If so, it is God's call for you to discover your lost inheritance.

What is the basic problem in our world today? Many human beings don't realize who they are. And if we don't know who we are and where we have come from, we will never become what we were meant to be. For an identity crisis will generate a self-acceptance crisis! But if we perceive ourselves as children of God, then he is our Father. We have an inheritance waiting for us. God has been waiting to find us. When that happens, we will be rid of our inferiority complex once and for all!

According to Greek legend, Helen of Troy was kidnapped and taken across the seas to a distant city where she suffered from amnesia and became a prostitute in the streets. She didn't know her name or that she was of royal blood.

Back in her homeland, friends didn't give up. One admiring adventurer believed she was alive and went to look for her. He never lost faith, and set off on a journey to find her.

One day he found himself wandering through the streets of a strange city. He came to a waterfront and saw a wretched woman with deep lines across her face and wearing tattered clothes. There was something about her that seemed familiar, so he walked up to her and asked, "What is your name?" She gave a name that was meaningless to him.

"Can I see your hands?" he asked. (He knew the lines in Helen's hands.) She held her hands out in front of her, and he gasped. "You are Helen! You are Helen of Troy! Do you remember?" She looked up at him in astonishment. "Helen!" he shouted. Then the fog seemed to clear, and a sense of recognition came to her face. Helen discovered her lost self, and she put her arms around her old friend and wept. Then Helen discarded the tattered clothes and once more became the queen she was born to be.

There is a widespread concept that the human being has evolved from an animal. If that's the case, if we are not children of God and if there is no God in heaven, then what? If that were true, then you and I can indeed feel inferior. And feelings of inferiority are the greatest threat to freedom. Then anybody who gains power—the political elite, the intellectual elite, the economical elite, the theological elite—can manipulate us.

It was said of the ancient Jews that they made terrible slaves because they were so proud and felt secure. By contrast, insecure, nonconfident, negative-self-imaged persons will quite naturally and easily surrender their freedom to the false security offered by the manipulative tactics of tyrannical persons or philosophies or powers.

The crucial political issue in the world today is theological—the doctrine of persons. Strip from humanity the doctrine of the divine origin of people and one can easily create a case for dictatorial rule by tyrannical powers—fascists of the right, or left—or rule by elitists.

Once we have lost sight of our divine heritage, we can expect to lose our freedom to political forces that will treat us like puppets, not like persons!

"Our Father in heaven, hallowed be your name," declares that we—human beings—are premium persons, not peasants or pawns. For we are children of God. We are members of the royal family!

Classical Reformed Theology declares that we are conceived and born rebellious sinners. But that answer is too shallow. It ignores the tough question: Why would love-needing persons resist, rebel against, and reject beautiful love? The answer? We are born nontrusting. Deep down we feel we are not good enough to approach a holy God. It is a perverted perfectionism that keeps us from coming close enough to God to believe in him.

It is precisely at this point that classical theology has erred in its insistence that theology be "God-centered," not "man-centered."

How can you possibly approach a person who feels inferior and unworthy with an invitation to believe in a holy God who hates sin and wants to punish the sinner? The answer? By introducing inferiority-plagued persons to a wonderful God-man named Jesus Christ who specializes in loving sinners.

What a great example of the glorious gospel the church has to proclaim! We have the theological/psychological therapy for persons who suffer from inferiority complexes because they make mistakes, because they are not perfect and don't know all the answers.

Are we to condemn ourselves for our mistakes? What's the answer? The ideal answer is to become a perfect person. If we could be perfect human beings, we'd have a sense of self-esteem. But you can't, and neither can I.

It is not until we meet Jesus Christ, who *is* perfect, and he offers to share his robe of righteousness with us and his garment of grace is draped across our shoulders that we can then walk with him into the presence of God (see Rom. 4). It is then that Jesus says, "Father, here's my new friend," and the Father says, "I love her. I love him. Come join my family." When that happens, we know that we are forgiven—we are treated like a perfect person even though we aren't, for the righteousness of Christ is credited to us. We are accepted as members of God's family.

Before we built our Crystal Cathedral, hundreds of overflow persons would have to sit outdoors each Sunday. During the wintertime hundreds of people would huddle together trying to keep warm. I still recall seeing a young lady offering to share her blanket with the person next to

her who was shivering in the cold. They moved close together as they worshiped God. It was a beautiful example
of family togetherness.

What is our hope? It is reconciliation. How can this happen? It will happen, I am convinced, when we redefine
our doctrine of sin.

Classical theology defines sin as "rebellion against God."
The answer is not incorrect as much as it is shallow and
insulting to the human being. Every person deserves to be
treated with dignity even if he or she is a "rebellious sinner." I suggest that the problem stems from a failure in
historical theology to make a distinction between "Adam's
sin" and "original sin." Adam was created in the image of
God and enjoyed at the outset of his human life a fellowship with the Father. Then "sin" entered the scene. What
was the sin? Bruce Larson has pointed out, "It was the
absence of total trust." Somehow Adam did not trust God's
promise for fulfillment enough to obediently abstain from
the forbidden fruit, and the immediate result of his diso-
bedience was guilt. And what is guilt but an ugly loss of
self-esteem? When God called, "Adam, where are you?"
Adam hid in the bushes.

While Adam was created "in fellowship" with God, all of
Adam's children were born detached from a trusting relationship with the heavenly Father. Their lives, unlike their
father's, started out not knowing God. They were born in
the jungle, disconnected, alienated, out-of-touch. Since
then, all of us were born nontrusting creatures of the jungle. The core of "original sin," that state in which we are all
born, is lack of trust.

Erik Erikson, the father of twentieth-century child psychiatry, helps us understand this when he tells us that
every child is born nontrusting. Lack of trust is another
way of saying that we are all born with a negative self-
image, an inferiority complex, if you please. We are therefore insecure persons by nature. This inherited inferiority

complex motivates us to manipulate a myriad mix of sub-conscious defense mechanisms designed to protect our deep-rooted insecurity from public exposure.

How subtly the wicked web is woven.

1. We withdraw from a belief in God for fear that our sins will be exposed, and we cannot stand the prospect of being embarrassed. So, doubt becomes an early defense mechanism of a nontrusting, guilty soul.

2. Since we are unable to throw off our natural religious instincts, we fabricate our own images of God. As insecure people, our natural fears take the face and form and force of anger. We appear to be mean, but actually, we are afraid. No wonder then that the unsaved human being imagines God to be angry rather than loving. The tangled web is becoming more complex.

3. We withdraw even further from a God that our fears have pictured as a threatening rather than a redeeming figure. The name of the true God of mercy who longs to save his children is not taken seriously.

4. We project these same patterns of human behavior to our other interpersonal relationships. Since we dare not trust, we lie. We are dishonest lest our imperfections be revealed. (Only self-esteeming persons dare to freely admit imperfections.) Coupled with this is an ever-recurring threat of boredom. We covet, hoping the conquest or the acquisitions will somehow give us the deep security we need. And often, adultery becomes the quick fix as it offers stimulation to the bored and a false sense of value or power to the ego-faltering philanderer.

If only we could love ourselves enough to dare approach God, what constructive dreams he would give us! What noble possibilities God wants to reveal to us—possibilities that would offer stimulation plus real security in service.

But we feel too unworthy. So one layer of negative behavior is laid upon another until we emerge as rebellious sinners. But our rebellion is a reaction, not our nature. By nature we are fearful, not bad. Original sin is not a mean streak; it is a nontrusting inclination.

The core of original sin, then is LOT—Lack of Trust. Or, it could be considered an innate inability to adequately value ourselves. Label it a "negative self-image," but do not say that the central core of the human soul is wickedness. If this were so, then truly, the human being is totally depraved. But positive Christianity does not hold to human depravity, but to human inability. I am humanly unable to correct my negative self-image until I encounter a life-changing experience with nonjudgmental love bestowed upon me by a Person whom I admire so much that to be unconditionally accepted by him is to be born again.

The golf ball may illustrate the nature of sin as explained above. If I were asked to define a golf ball and described it merely as a round white ball, I would not be incorrect; I would simply lack in-depth analysis. That is the way it would be if I call sin simply "rebellion against God." The outside of the golf ball is made up of a thin, but hard, dimpled cover—usually white. Rebellion is merely the outer cover, the externality of sin. The core of the golf ball is hard. And the core of sin is a negative self-image, around which are the stretched-maze of negative reactions. The body of the golf ball is a maze of stretched rubber wrappings. The negative self-image forms the hidden core from which emerges the anxieties,

fears, and negative emotions that finally present a face that appears to be angry, mean, rebellious. The truth is, however, that the human being at the deepest level is afraid, nontrusting, insecure, terribly defensive.

To be born again means that we must be changed from a negative to a positive self-image—from inferiority to self-esteem, from fear to love, from doubt to trust.

How can this happen? It happens through a meeting with the Ideal One. From my perspective I would expect such an Ideal One to ignore or reject me because of my own shortcomings. But if in fact the Ideal One receives me as his peer and treats me as an equal even though he knows who and what I am—the ill I've done and the good I've failed to do—then something profoundly deep will happen at the core of my personality. I will be born again. For if I know that he knows me and yet treats me like his equal, I will have a life-transforming experience with non-judgmental love (saving grace), and I'll be able to *trust* and be liberated to love. The fears that have kept me from daring to love will be gone. For the first time I will dare to come out of the bushes and meet my heavenly Father without fear of rejection. I will dare to accept and experience reconciliation.

Can you imagine any psychological or psychiatric therapy that can begin to approach the healing power of this religious experience? Can you imagine the healing power of an unconditional love between the Ideal One (Jesus) and a rebellious human who is suffering from insecurity, defensiveness, and feelings of inferiority?

Now—by the grace of Christ I am introduced to my Heavenly Father. If Christ—the Ideal One—(1) accepts me, (2) forgives me, (3) assures me that God is my Father and it's safe to draw near to the Heavenly Father, (4) announces to me that God wants to *use me* in a beautiful work of sharing Christian love in this world—then truly I am being deeply, positively transformed!

Now I can say with St. Paul, "I can do all things through Christ who strengthens me." When we have been redeemed into God's family, we are ready to think big—as God thinks. And we are ready to dream that great divine dream of building the kingdom of God in the world. Healed of our feelings of inferiority by our identification with the family of God, we suddenly begin to be released from the negative self-image which would keep us from daring or deserving to think big and beautiful as God wants every human being to think.

The "I am" will determine the "I can."

Self-Esteem will lead us to possibility thinking.

When we are adopted as children of God, the core of our life changes from shame—to self-esteem.

And we can pray, "Our Father in heaven, honorable is *our* name."

So, the foundation is laid for us to feel good about ourselves! The stage is set for important divine marching orders!

Chapter Five

The Divine Design
for Human Dignity

"YOUR KINGDOM COME, your will be done on earth as it is in heaven." In this single sentence there rises a hope for every human being to discover the lost glory his heart desires.

I hold the promise that I might be able to be *someone* for somebody. The deep longing to be needed must be met before I will be able to discover my value. Human dignity emerges in redemptive relationships. So, a theology of self-esteem sets the stage where a theology of social ethics will evolve naturally, unavoidably, beautifully.

Surely, in a world where so many persons are lonely and hurting, there's no excuse for anyone not feeling needed. It's no wonder that real Christians really feel good about themselves, for the born-again believer has an incurable compulsion to love people. And love is my deciding to make your problem my problem. This is what God did on the Cross of Christ.

Authentic love will motivate us to *get involved*. And real self-affirmation becomes the path to self-denial. The "I am" will always determine the "I can." If I am God's child, I can believe that I can do "something beautiful for God," to use Mother Teresa's favorite phrase. Gladly I'll take up the cross of personal involvement in someone else's problems with the result that I will feel needed, and the warm glow of self-esteem will be my reward. Self-affirmation and self-esteem inspire sacrificial service which generates fresh self-worth. I call this self-esteem recycled.

That, in summary, is the lesson of this chapter. That, in brief, is what we can expect if we dare to pray, "Your kingdom come, your will be done": God will give us a human need-filling dream to feed our self-esteem.

We think bigger, more beautifully, with loftier dreams. And we find that as we dream of an exciting kingdom controlled by the gracious will of a wonderful God, the depression of personal insignificance and meaninglessness and purposelessness in life disappears like the fog dissipates in the noonday sun. *Dreams dispel depression and discouragement.*

"Your kingdom come, your will be done on earth as it is in heaven." How does this petition dispel depression and discouragement? Five theological position-statements may answer that question.

1. *God has a self-esteem-building plan for the human race and this runs through human history.* This master plan of God is designed around the deepest needs of human beings—self-dignity, self-respect, self-worth, self-esteem. God envisions a kingdom where the human value of self-esteem will affect psychology, law, art, ethics, economics, politics, science, and literature.

Now, just what is the meaning of "God's kingdom on earth as it is in heaven"? All human kingdoms are built around the ego and power-hungry motivations of people who are inwardly insecure and have a craving for neurotic power. What they are really doing is clumsily trying to find the pearl of great price—genuine self-respect and self-esteem! And in an effort to feed their frail self-image, they will manipulate, dominate, control, and exploit their fellow human beings. Because they violate the self-dignity of other people while they manipulate their personal power, these insecure, power-pursuing persons generate no authentic self-esteem for themselves. *And, no person can really love himself unless and until he builds and boosts the self-worth of others.*

God's kingdom, by contrast, is a society where the divine spirit of self-respect and self-esteem penetrates the substance, style, strategy, and spirit of human interactions and interrelationships. The self-esteem of each person is accepted unconditionally and irrevocably as that human value which will control all of life.

What is the kingdom of God on earth? It is a community of persons who, through an experience of nonjudgmental acceptance and affirmation by Jesus Christ, have been personally redeemed from self-shame to self-esteem. This rebirth of self-worth becomes their divine compulsion. This "new life within" expresses itself in a prosocial behavior. In private and in community the drive to release our self-esteem results in a new standard of social conduct for all of the world to behold. Even as it is the nature of a seed to sprout, it is the nature of love to give itself away, and it is the nature of self-esteem to treat others with respect. So, the kingdom of God is a noninstitutionalized divine organism that positively infects the secular society. "It is no longer I who live, but Christ who lives in me"—inspiring us to treat all human beings as "first-class" passengers on this space craft called Planet Earth.

When we pray, "Thy kingdom come," we are praying for the successful growth, the prospering enlargement, of the increase of the number of redeemed people, looking to the day when human beings will be inspired by kingdom persons to treat one another with respect and dignity regardless of race, religion, economic class, or politics. Jesus, when he confronted secular unbelievers as well as conspicuous sinners, still refrained from insulting or embarrassing them. He left their dignity intact.

2. *God's plan includes all who choose to be included.* No person is too insignificant to be used by God. Everyone who does some act that builds self-esteem and self-respect in other persons is at least a silent ally, if not in fact a committed member of God's kingdom. And his kingdom is coming and his will is being done every time we act in a way that lifts another person's dignity.

I met her during the six months my fourteen-year-old daughter was in the hospital recovering from the amputation of her leg after a terrible motorcycle accident. She was a refugee from Vietnam and did not speak English. She had the most menial job in the hospital—emptying the waste baskets. But each time she passed my daughter's bed, she'd stop and smile. Love radiated from her face, and that helped our feverish little girl. Love is the international language that builds self-esteem. No person is so ignorant, so uneducated, so lacking in talent or beauty that he or she is incapable of becoming a really love-sharing person.

Someone sent me a copy of the last will and testament of a poor laborer who lived long ago in Germany. In his final bequest he wrote, "I leave my eldest son my most prized possession, the tool that I used to cut the stone for the Cologne Cathedral!" That humble mason found self-esteem and pride in his work. He felt included in the purposes of God.

3. *God's plan for our life will come to us in a dream that will build our self-esteem.* This touches upon what I consider to be one of the major flaws in many a Christian life. Frequently, Christians experience an inspiring thought or dream that is loaded with possibilities. We experience an exciting idea, but because possibilities feed our self-esteem and hint at potential personal ego-fulfillment, we suspect it is a contradiction to Christian humility. In a pietistic, negative reaction we discard the idea and repress our de-

sires, not realizing that this was in fact God's dream for our self-esteem. It is terribly important that we never reject a good idea simply because it might feed our normal ego needs. "It is God who works in you, inspiring both the will and the deed, for his own chosen purpose" (Phil. 2:13, NEB).

"Don't worry about humility. The easiest job for God to do is to keep you and me humble. God's biggest job is to get us to believe that we *are* somebody and that we really can *do* something." This is a message I find I must constantly restate: "Enjoy the pride of your inheritance." We are to enjoy the good feeling that comes when we sense that God wants to use us. Remember, "If your pride is rooted in your divine call, your humility is assured. The Cross will sanctify your ego trip."

4. *The Cross is the central force in the kingdom of God.* What part does the Cross play in the building up of the kingdom of God? The answer must be viewed from both the Cross of Christ and the cross of the Christian.

The death of Christ on the cross is central to our salvation. It is God's price tag on a human soul. If "Christ died for me," I must be of infinite value in God's sight. In addition, the Cross declares that God is capable of forgiving any sin. On the cross Jesus prayed, "Father, forgive them." If God can forgive those who executed his Son, if this marvelous Jesus, victim of his personal holocaust, can plead for mercy for his executioners, then God can forgive me too! I can be saved from the self-esteem-polluting guilt of my sin! Christ's Cross makes my salvation possible. It sets a self-esteem-setting standard for his sacred society. I am now inspired to forgive those who would crucify me too!

"God loves you and so do I" is more than just a slogan. It is a proud, positive proclamation of the Cross—the vertical and the horizontal intersection of a relationship with God and a relationship with those around me. The Cross is the divine-human intersection. God gives my self-respect a boost with his nonjudgmental love. I must do the same for my fellow humans. I must get involved. I must accept the dream God gives me and develop its inherent possibilities. The price of any dream is always self-denial, the voluntary vicarious assumption of the Cross. Pursuing possibility thinking is the way of the Cross. Make no mistake about that.

When God's dream is accepted, we must be prepared to pay a high price. The dream that comes from God calls us to fulfill his will by taking an active part in his kingdom. The price? A cross. The reward? A feeling of having done something beautiful for God! But the path will lead us through the valley of potential humiliation before the crown of godly pride is placed upon our heads. That in part is what the Cross means.

If God is interested in self-esteem, why would he let Jesus die a shameful death on a cross? Was Christ's self-esteem being fulfilled when he hung naked on a cross? That question should be contemplated alongside this theological statement: *The Cross sanctifies the ego trip.* For the Cross protected our Lord's perfect self-esteem from turning into sinful pride. Jesus said, "I, if I be lifted up . . . will draw all men unto me" (John 12:32, KJV). His plan was glorious. His sense of success was assured. Jesus knew he would win the attention of the world. And he has! Yet what could be misinterpreted as proud boasting was perfected through the humiliation of the Cross.

There is no self-esteem without sacrifice. There is no sacrifice without being exposed to the possibility of ridicule. There's no way we can pursue a dream without running the risk of people saying, "Who does he think he is?"

What separates dangerous egotism from healthy self-esteem? The difference is the cross we are willing to bear to fulfill God's will. The cross is the price we will have to pay to succeed, i.e., to realize the inspiring dream God has given us. Before God can give us the crown (grand and glorious pride), he will call us to a dream that is demanding. God will not destroy our ego; he will redeem it. Our ego will be sanctified through our cross and shall emerge as humble but happy self-esteem! There is no success without a cross. There is no gain without pain.

5. *God's will and plan for his kingdom is ultimate success.* God will see us through to ultimate success, so self-esteem generates possibility thinking. The "I am" inspires an "I can."

Mother Teresa of Calcutta had a dream. She told her superiors, "I have three pennies and a dream from God to build an orphanage."

"Mother Teresa," her superiors chided gently, "you cannot build an orphanage with three pennies. With three pennies, you can't do anything."

"I know," she said, smiling, "but with God and three pennies I can do anything!"

Mother Teresa has become an international symbol of real success.

But, what is ultimate success? I hold that success is experiencing the self-esteem that arises deep within us when we build it in others through sincere self-denial and sacrificial service. To build self-esteem in others is to walk in God's will and do his work. To build self-worth in another person is the fulfillment of the prayer, "Thy kingdom come, thy will be done."

Success, then, must not be perceived as "always winning and never losing." It is not to be defined as "reaching all my goals on time." Rather, success is to be defined as the gift of self-esteem that God gives us as a reward for our sacrificial service in building self-esteem in others. Win or lose: If we follow God's plan as faithfully as we can, we will feel good about ourselves. That is success! We will then be able to live with ourselves with dignity when we know deep down in our hearts that we did what God wanted us to do.

The Christian is on an integrity trip, not an ego trip. And if we are faithful to our divine call, we make the great discovery—our integrity fulfills our ego needs. So even if we fail, we can feel great, for we know we did what we had to do—we had to try. Over the years I've taught one of my favorite slogans to more than a million people, "I'd rather attempt to do something great and fail, than attempt to do nothing and succeed."

Chapter Six

Invalidism or Individualism

THE LORD'S PRAYER is emerging now as a classic, timeless therapy for the universal restlessness in the human mind that deprives persons from really feeling good about themselves.

Here is the pathway to peace of mind revealed to the human race by Christ. Like the laws of physics or mathematics that are to be learned by each new generation, the Lord's Prayer is passed down to us as from teacher to student. Here in this prayer are the spiritual truths that unlock serenity of soul. Like modern students in geography and astronomy who memorize maps that were well-charted decades or centuries ago, we shall discover the timeless spiritual truths and can generate great personal awareness of personal worth.

There are ancient arts and crafts that have passed the test of time and can be embraced, preserved, and passed on from age to age. But tragically, these can in fact also be carelessly, casually, or cynically ignored or ridiculed by the next generation, only to be lost to join the tragic roll call of "lost arts."

Have wise and perceptive students and teachers of spiritual truth discovered long ago the cure to the classical emotional ailments that assail the normal human being? And is our generation—and each new generation—tempted and inclined to arrogantly imagine that we will be the first discoverers, analysts, and prescribers of cures and therapies for mental, psychological, and emotional disturbances?

Continue to approach, my reader friend, humbly and respectfully, the prayer couch of Jesus Christ. For here, centuries before Freud or Adler or Frankl, is the great revelation that can meet our deepest human needs. The therapy? Call it prayer therapy. The ageless, timeless, proven healing power? The Lord's Prayer. Let me summarize now what we have discovered in the previous chapters of this book.

1. We can replace inferiority complexes with a new self-image, one with divine roots. God is my Father; "I am somebody!"

2. We can then release dynamic possibility thinking for constructive, creative living. The awareness of our divine roots will inspire the pursuits of divine fruits. We will be caught up in a vision of a cause, a crusade, a divine calling. We will sense a high and honorable purpose for life, and we will accept God's invitation to play our important part in the kingdom he is busily creating NOW in this world. God needs you and me to help create a society of self-esteeming people. We will expect to succeed. For God is not planning our failure.

3. Next, we must and will be shielded from the destructive effects of *anxiety*. The third negative emotion, anxiety, can be a paralyzing, depressing, stifling, and ultimately defeating negative emotion. Anxiety is dealt with in this simple line, "Give us this day our daily bread." Why be anxious when God will supply our needs? God may not

give us everything we want, but he'll always give us what we really need.

TRUST FOR THE CRUST

"Give us this day our daily bread." What does the word *bread* mean? Bread refers to life's basic needs. God doesn't promise that we will get the dessert, but he does promise that we will have the crust. That which we must have, we will have. We need air to breathe, water to drink, and we must have a crust of bread to live. And so we must trust God for the crust. What we need, God will provide.

When God gives us what we need, it seldom seems like such a noteworthy thing. The basic necessities of life are seldom flashy or flamboyant. What's showy about a crust of bread? Yet it is this very thing that sustains our life. Jesus came quietly into the world without fanfare, without trumpets, without a grand parade—a simple baby born in a manger among the cattle. And yet, he said, "I am the bread of life." The crust didn't seem to have much class.

What is the crust that God offers? We call it possibility thinking. It is nothing more than a process of thinking that is stimulated and sustained by trust. That's what you and I need. And when God gives us the best, he never gives us a thing—but always a thought!

Things wear out, rust, go out of style, but thoughts are eternal. Things do not build self-esteem, but thoughts that inspire the creation of beautiful things can produce a healthy pride.

God's ultimate objective is to turn you and me into self-confident persons. And only self-confident persons become leaders capable of creating a self-esteeming society.

Material things, of course, do not build self-confident persons. Self-esteem that is rooted in materialistic status symbols (we need not elaborate) has a short life span. Fashions change quickly, but self-confidence rooted in sincere and sacrificial service, in answer to God's Cross-centered call, is sure to bring ultimate satisfaction.

So, God's solution to the poverty problem is to stab at the root, not the surface fruit of the problem. What is so bad about poverty? Not having shoes, shirts, or a beautiful home? I know too many super-rich kids who, in the balmy climates of California and Hawaii, reject the big house, the shoes, and fancy shirts and choose to live with only one tattered pair of jeans and sandals without socks. Why? They have missed the joys of real self-esteem in our materialistic culture. Are they overreacting? Quite possibly. But what is bad about poverty is that at its worst it leaves persons without any self-respect. Real, abject poverty strips a human being of his dignity. He can, and often does, regress negatively until, losing consciousness of his divine calling, he becomes an animal.

And so we ask, how can we eliminate poverty in such a way that we eliminate the worst element in poverty—loss of dignity? How do we replace the loss of self-esteem in the very poor with what they need most of all—dignity, self-esteem, self-confidence, noble achievement, pride of accomplishment, pride of ownership? This can happen by giving them thoughts before things.

The real reason materialism ultimately fails is because its doctrine and theology of persons is in error. Materialism interprets persons and pressures in materialistic terms so it offers superficial solutions which too often are counterproductive. Too often the welfare check deprives people of dignity and makes them feel dependent. It robs them of the courage to try. They do not dare to risk failure even though it is the only way to achieve genuine self-esteem. If God would rain dollars from heaven to remove poverty from the face of the earth, the deeper plague of poverty would still persist.

If all persons were given financial security, would they

automatically be internally secure? No. They would then need not fear financial problems. But the absence of fear is no indication of courage. Courage can only come through experiences where we run a risk, take a chance—we win some and we lose some. And in the process we emerge brave people, brave enough to lose if need be.

When God gives us creative ideas, they are always risky, but in the process, he is feeding our self-esteem and lifting us from internal poverty. Consequently, what people need today, more than welfare checks or hand-outs, are thoughts—opportunity-revealing, possibility-thinking thoughts!

Without these positive thoughts, all the material accumulations are worthless. That's why it is not uncommon to find people who are healthy, have good connections, possess power and wealth, and yet still end up committing suicide. You and I can have everything, but if we don't have new-possibility ideas that fill our lives with fresh, youthful enthusiasm and pride-producing purpose, everything we have will soon turn to dust and ashes.

"Give us this day our daily bread." God will give us what we need. And what is that? It is creative, inspiring, possibility-pregnant ideas. We need those God-inspired thoughts when we face the problems of life. The crust of bread will be the thought from God that says, "Do not quit," for with his help we will see the possibility of victory in the toughest times.

Christ is my "crust of bread." He gives me the ideas, and so instead of being overwhelmed when I'm faced with a problem, the problem turns into an opportunity. Tears turn into pearls. Scars turn into stars. The difficulties begin to yield dividends. Gain rises from the pain.

It is so easy to undervalue the ideas God gives us even as we tend to undervalue a crust of bread. But by giving us creative ideas, God feeds our self-esteem while he lifts us from poverty and need. And in so doing we come to see that even if we could redistribute the world wealth so that everyone had enough, the deeper plague of poverty would still persist. For the plague of poverty is shame, loss of pride, loss of dignity and self-esteem. Dignity is not born and sustained by charity.

PRIDE OF OWNERSHIP—PRIDE OF EARNERSHIP

If real poverty is indeed loss of dignity, and if materialistic accumulation does not equate true wealth, then how is self-esteem acquired, dignity instilled, and emotional and spiritual wealth restored? The answer lies in the deceptively simple phrase, "Give us this day our daily bread, our crust of bread—life-sustaining ideas." These positive thoughts, fresh ideas, and new dreams are the beginning of the process of dignity-rejuvenation. God-given ideas will challenge and equip us to rise from poverty to pride. As we grasp the ideas, pursue the challenges, and realize success, we can discover the pride of earnership as well as the pride of ownership.

This principle became real to me one day when I met a truly remarkable man. Dashing out of an elegant hotel lobby, I hailed a roving taxicab, and as we moved away from the curb, I settled into the seat and began to rehearse in my mind the lecture I was about to give. Suddenly, the driver turned and enthusiastically asked, "Dr. Schuller?"

I looked up into the face of an animated young black man. The gold ring that pierced his nose intrigued me. "Yes, I'm he."

"You saved my life!"

"I did? Tell me how."

"I was born and raised in Harlem. And for many years I lived on welfare. I couldn't hold down a job because I never thought I was good enough at anything for anyone to hire me.

"Then I heard you on 'Hour of Power.' You really made me think that I could do something, so I called the taxi company and asked if they would hire me. Then they asked me if I'd be willing to drive a cab in Harlem. Of course, I was willing. Apparently they were having trouble finding a driver who would work Harlem. So, I was hired.

"It's great! I'm no longer on welfare. The food my family and I eat is food I earned. I've earned everything we own."

This vibrant young man didn't have just the pride of ownership, he also possessed the pride of earnership. God didn't give him things, he gave him an idea. And when we have the right ideas, even though we may lack material wealth, the right thoughts will produce everything we need, including money, for money in a free economy flows to great ideas.

When God gives you your daily bread, he provides everything you need, not only money, or food and clothing, or ideas. But he also provides the stamina and the strength to turn those ideas into realities. When we face difficulties, God will supply the crust of bread with the thought, "Do not quit." And he helps us see the possibility of victory in the toughest times.

Christ is my "crust of bread." He gives me the ideas, the motivation, and the ability to overcome difficulties. Problems turn into opportunities. So instead of being overwhelmed when I'm faced with a problem, I am able to overwhelm my problems. The difficulties begin to yield dividends. Gain rises from the pain.

Achievement in spite of obstacles yields dignity and self-respect. Yet, because the ideas are God-given, the sense of achievement contains an innate humility. There is no way any self-respecting person will become egotistical when he realizes his success depends upon ideas that come from God. What a brilliant and balanced solution—God gives thoughts, not things, and consequently there is humility without humiliation, self-esteem without arrogance.

God gives his ideas to everyone. Yet some people close their ears to them, while others hear them but are afraid to act upon those ideas or to believe in them. Did you know that the difference between the super-success, the moderate-success, and the loser is not a matter of talent, training, or territory? It is a matter of *trust.*

At the bottom of every ladder, there is a crowd of talented, trained people with academic degrees and credentials who can drop names and claim connections, but they aren't going anywhere. Really, success is not a matter of talent, training, territory as much as it is the skillful and prayerful management of divinely-inspired ideas.

The difference between the people at the top of the ladder and those at the middle and the bottom is so basic. The people at the top have learned how to handle good ideas, but those who stay in the middle or at the bottom of the ladder have never learned to hatch, harbor, and handle creative thoughts.

Some people never learn how to relate to other people effectively, and they always have problems in relationships. They can't handle people. Some people never learn how to handle money, and they always have financial problems. Others have never learned how to manage positive ideas, so they never achieve their potential.

God builds our self-image by giving us the wisdom to manage the positive ideas that he sends our way. His response to our deep needs are—ideas, dreams, hopes, and inspirations. These are the crust, the daily bread, that will ultimately feed our self-esteem. Do not doubt their potential power. Trust the crust that comes from God. "Trust in the Lord, and do good; so you will dwell in the land and enjoy security. Take delight in the Lord, and he will give you the desires of your heart" (Ps. 37:3–4).

But now we must face a crucial question. Are we suspicious of trust as a life principle? Many secular cynics would suggest that trust is the hallmark of the gullible. *Psychology Today* published a significant study entitled,

"Trust and Its Consequences."[1] The study reported the work of Dr. Julian Rotter from the University of Connecticut, who for many years has studied trust and its consequences on human behavior and personality development. He developed a scale of thirty-five questions which determine whether a person is a high-, middle-, or low-trusting person. He then took high-trusting, low-trusting, and middle-trusting persons and had their IQ's and other behavioral patterns tested. Based on his research and reports, I have created a little true or false test that I'm going to give you now.

1. True or False: Trusting persons tend to be more gullible. (Answer: false) Quite the opposite is true. Trusting persons appear intuitively to prepare themselves for extreme, irresponsible—call it gullible—reactions as they move forward positively.

2. True or False: Trusting persons tend to have a lower IQ than skeptical people. (Answer: false) Trusting persons have as high an IQ as the skeptics.

3. True or False: Trusting persons live happier lives than nontrusting persons. (Answer: true) Of course! They have the capacity to discover the reality of God.

4. True or False: Trusting persons tend to be more trustworthy than nontrusting persons. (Answer: true)

5. True or False: The trusting person is more likely to fall for the con artist. (Answer: false) Studies show that the trusting person is actually less susceptible to a rip-off artist.

What the study suggests is this pragmatic possibility: the trusting person is healthy; the nontrusting is unhealthy. *As the birds were created to fly and the fish to swim, human beings were created to breathe the air of trust and exhale the pollution of doubt.* We were designed to breathe in faith and exhale cynicism. In our natural emotional habitat and healthy state of mind, we were created to be trusting persons.

To understand this principle better, let's look at the clinically acceptable definition of health and of sickness.

The key word to understanding and defining health is "function." A body that is healthy is functioning properly. A sick body is not functioning properly. Now with that simple definition, we see that the nontrusting person is not functioning properly; he is therefore sick. On the other hand the trusting person is functioning properly, and is living an emotionally healthy life.

Next we come to the real question: *Why did God create the human being to be a trusting person?* After all, isn't trusting taking a chance? If you can be sure of something, it doesn't involve trust. What is God's reason behind the scheme of trusting? Or, to put it another way, "What is the thrust behind the trust?"

We can discover the answer to these questions when we examine the nature of the human race. There are basically two kinds of persons: those who are individuals and others who are really invalids. I refer to this as "individualism" and "invalidism." As we look at all institutions, religious, political, economic, or social, we find that they are made up of people who either lean towards *individualism* or towards *invalidism*.

What is invalidism? It is the system that keeps a person from discovering his or her own potential. An *invalid* is a sick person who is not functioning properly at his or her peak potential. Lack of trust produces and promotes invalidism.

In contrast, trust produces individualism. *Individuals* are people who are healthy and are developing the potential that God created within them. They are discovering their possibilities and are enjoying a rising self-dignity in the process. They are worshiping and glorifying God and are becoming the individuals that he meant them to be. Self-confident, redeemed persons are individuals, not invalids.

God created the trust system with the intent that we would develop fully as individuals, for it is *the trust system that turns invalids into individuals*. The ultimate invalid is the newborn infant. Erik Erikson has taught us that in the first stage of a child's life, from birth to twelve months, the infant learns only one thing, and that is *trust*. I don't suppose there is a hospital today where nurses are not taught to stroke and talk to the premature infant in a way that communicates trust. This therapy is based on Erikson's teaching that the newborn infant is born nontrusting. Birth is a traumatic experience, and the infant must learn to live detached from the womb as an individual. With this understanding, we can go so far as to say that we can detect emotional immaturity and infantilism by a person's incapacity to trust. *We can measure the maturity and adulthood of a human being by the level that he rises to in his capacity to trust.*

Many of our contemporary social structures and systems exploit a person's natural inclination to remain an invalid all of his life. Political, social, and even religious institutions have on occasion exploited the nontrusting inclination of a person by offering so much security that he won't have to face risk or danger. This only perpetuates invalidism, because in this manipulative arrangement the person really doesn't need to develop trust. Political promises offer to take care of people from the cradle to the grave. Even some forms of Christianity are inaccurate in turning their religion into a hospital instead of a physical-fitness center. When I was a child, I learned to love this hymn:

> Be not dismayed, whate'er betide,
> God will take care of you;
> Beneath His wings of love abide,
> God will take care of you.

This is a good theology when understood in the right context, but if distorted, people simply think God will take care of them. Yet the song says, "Beneath His wings of love abide." This means beneath the wings of God's love, we can go out, take a chance, and run the risk.

Trust in God's scheme of throwing us out of the nest until we have to learn to fly. There's a great verse in the Bible that says, "Like an eagle that stirs up its nest, that flutters over its young, spreading out its wings, catching them . . ." (Deut. 32:11). The thrust behind the trust is very simple. When we are forced to stand on our own two feet with no guarantee that the government or anyone else will rescue us, then we will have to trust the hidden possibilities that the Creator has built within every person. Trusting persons become adventuring people, and adventuring people discover that when they take a chance, together with God, excitement occurs. As energy is produced and success is realized, then the ultimate prize is in store. They realize, "I am an individual!"

This feeling of independence and self-esteem is ultimately what we all desire. Deep down in our hearts we do not want to feel totally dependent on others. Trust makes all the difference in the world. When we follow God's scheme of trust, we turn from an invalid into an individual. We begin to attempt the impossible and obtain our heart's real desire—self-esteem, self-respect, self-affirmation, self-confidence. And that spells freedom, as we become free from dependence on others. That's the thrust behind the trust. *God pushes us out in faith so that we can discover who we are and what we can do and be as individuals.*

In this context consider this claim of Christ: "I am the Bread of Life." The question I must ask myself and challenge others to ask is: Have I ever in my life sincerely said, "Jesus Christ, I accept you as my Savior and Lord"?

The Lordship of Christ is certain to be a positive self-dignity-generating experience. For Christ calls us to trust his friendship and his fellowship. In his presence possibilities explode, creativity flourishes, and challenges emerge as his love flows through us. Risks appear with the rising opportunities.

So, Christ becomes the crust of bread that will meet our deepest needs. Beautiful thoughts start flowing through

the mind connected to a heart that has received Christ as
Lord and Savior.

And in accepting me, in forgiving me, Christ cleanses
me of guilt. And the result is: I feel positive about myself.
In accepting him as my Lord, I know he'll call me to some
service of love. I'll find my niche in his kingdom-building
work today. I'll start treating people the way Christ treats
me. And I can feel the self-esteem rising all around me
and within me, "Rivers of living water shall flow from the
inmost being of anyone who believes in me" (John 7:38,
TLB). I'll really feel good about myself. And it all started
with a crust called Christ, my Bread of life! It begins when
we trust God for the crust.

Chapter Seven

God's Prescription
for Emotional Health

WE ARE REALLY discovering, aren't we, that the Lord's Prayer, in one short paragraph, has the message that meets the deepest needs of the human heart.

No psychiatrist, psychologist, philosopher, behavioral-modification expert—no counselor, no therapist, has ever written a paragraph that deals such a blow to the six basic negative emotions that rob people of their emotional stability and well-being: 1) Inferiority, 2) Meaninglessness, 3) Anxiety, 4) Guilt, 5) Resentment, 6) Fear.

"Our Father, in heaven, hallowed be your name." If God is my Father and I belong to his family, then I AM SOMEBODY. This erases my inferiority feelings once and for all, and I have a solid spiritual foundation for the birth of a positive self-image.

> "I may be young; I may be old,"
>   But I am somebody,
>   For I am God's child.
> "I may be educated; I may be unlettered,"
>   But I am somebody,
>   For I am God's child.
> "I may be black; I may be white,"

But I am somebody,
For I am God's child.
"I may be rich; I may be poor,"
But I am somebody,
For I am God's child.
"I may be fat; I may be thin,"
But I am somebody,
For I am God's child.
"I may be married; I may be divorced,"
But I am somebody,
For I am God's child.
"I may be successful; I may be a failure,"
But I am somebody,
For I am God's child.
"I may be a sinner; I may be a saint,"
But I am somebody,
For Jesus is my Savior.
I am God's child!

Because "I am" somebody, "I can" do more than I ever thought I could.

The second negative emotion which we must confront is meaninglessness which often takes the form of despair, depression, discouragement, or existential loneliness. The condition is addressed in the second sentence of the Lord's Prayer: "Your kingdom come, your will be done on earth as it is in heaven." This is another way of saying, God has a plan and it includes me, for I am somebody! If God's plan includes me, then I will have the self-esteem that will inspire me to dream. Most people fail to dream because creative desires, daring dreams, and dynamic imaginings are aborted before birth by a subconscious fear of failure. And what is fear of failure? It is a lack of self-confidence born from a too-low self-esteem.

What we need desperately is the courage to overcome the fear of failure. So the next petition in the Lord's Prayer is helpful here: "Give us this day our daily bread." I shall trust God to give me the success to match the dream he has given me. I must believe he will give me a miracle to match my mountain. I can expect obstacles, barriers, and walls that threaten to thwart my pursuits, but I believe God will help me climb the wall if I'll answer his call. He will solve the obviously impossible problems after I've made the daring decision to try—that is trust! "My God will supply every need of yours . . . in Christ Jesus" (Phil. 4:19).

When we reach this new state of spiritual consciousness, when our self-worth reaches this level of healthy awareness, will we really feel good about ourselves? Or will our renewed condition only give rise to new conflicts? Quite possibly we can expect a sudden surge of new guilt. For if we are a special creation of God and if we are part of his family, and if he has a creative dream for our lives, if he promises that he'll give us what we need to make us succeed, then can you imagine what opportunities we've neglected in our lifetimes? Can you imagine how often we've missed the mark? How many deeds of mercy we have left undone? What bright ideas have passed through our brain that we've let go as if we were standing at the railing of an ocean liner and somebody poured diamonds into our hands and we watched them fall through our fingers into the sea, never to be caught again?

My friend Fred Smith of Dallas expressed it like this: "You know what hell would be for me? This is what hell would be: If, when I stand before God, he would tell me all the things I could have done in my life if I had only had more faith." I agree, it would be hell if God ever told me all of the "diamond ideas" that I have allowed to flow wastefully through my brain. It would be hell if God ever told me of the beautiful relationships I could have had if only I'd had more courage, or more patience. It would be hell if God told me all of the accomplishments I could have achieved in life if I had been willing to pay the price. It would be hell if God should tell me all of the possibilities I wasted. It would be hell if God showed me how I could have succeeded if I'd only tried, if I had not quit, and if I'd just hung on a little longer. "The saddest words of tongue or pen are these—it might have been."

This makes the theology of possibility thinking profoundly significant. For no human being will accomplish the ultimate objective of real Christianity without possibility thinking.

What, after all, is the basic obligation of every Christian? What is the ultimate objective of the most serious theological declaration? What is the divine purpose of persons on planet earth? All solid, serious theological statements drawn from Scripture agree: The human being's purpose is to worship God and glorify him. Very true. But this is too shallow until we probe the dangerous question: how can we mortals worship God and glorify him? The answer, I believe, is by doing his work, by walking his walk, and by following his will—our work must be our worship.

THE WORK ETHIC IS MY WORTH EPIC

The work ethic rightly understood is a prescription for self-worth. Ultimately all human effort, must be (1) released from fear of failure; (2) viewed as an opportunity to carry out God's plan for our lives; (3) controlled by a pursuit of excellence. As the true story of human labor unfolds, we can see that the "work ethic is a person's self-worth epic."

A friend of mine in Kasmir, India, is an astute businessman. He deals in hand-carved furniture, and his company motto is "Work Is Worship!" No wonder his quality of product is superlative.

That is profound theology with incredible practical results for society. And it is no wonder that persons whose self-esteem generates possibility thinking are also the persons who get involved in projects that have high commitment to integrity and excellence. The motivation to honest labor and noble achievement is rooted in our redemption, and the pursuit of excellence is the natural result.

Every positive possibility idea is a trust, not a treasure. As a possibility thinker, I am God's steward, not the private owner of opportunities. Consequently, it is my before-God-accountable-responsibility to discover and develop the hidden possibilities in every positive idea until the highest and holiest potentials have emerged from these God-given ideas and possibilities. Then, as an act of constructive, creative, praise and worship, I return the idea-turned-achievement (hopefully without spot or wrinkle) back to God to glorify him.

And what is my reward? It is the gift of divine grace—"A wonderful feeling of divine self-esteem." So the work *ethic* becomes my worth *epic*.

This compulsion to excellence, then, is driven by our spiritual self-esteem. "I am God's child entrusted with God's idea so I must excel! I must not settle for mediocrity." This pursuit of excellence is fantastic—but potentially dangerous if it leads to unrealistic perfectionism. Perfectionism is unrealistic excellence which produces guilt. How do we solve this problem? How do we avoid the guilt of perfectionism without defusing the drive to excellence? The answer: "By inserting the concept of forgiveness!" So God dropped into its proper place in this prayer the next healing sentence: "Forgive us our debts as we forgive our debtors."

Forgiving is living. We'll take a giant step up the let's-feel-good-about-ourselves-ladder when we experience the profoundly positive, regenerating, rejuvenating, revitalizing peace, love, and joy that is the emotional reward of the person who receives and offers forgiveness.

We need not elaborate further on the pains and perils of that emotional pollution called guilt and its Siamese twin—

resentment. This is the heart of hell on earth. Let me only add what may be the most serious consequence and the least understood and the most neglected in Christian theological literature. I refer to the devastating effect unforgiven guilt and nursed and nurtured resentments have on our most prized possession—our most treasured gem, the most valued of human values—our self-respect, our self-esteem.

Consider thoughtfully and prayerfully how resentments, handled positively, can bolster our self-respect. Resentments harbored and then released in verbal violence or negative antisocial behavior may make us feel good at the moment as we release our anger, hatred, or vengeance. Why? Simply because our frustration is released. On a lower level our price has been vindicated. But on a far higher level our self-esteem, our "Christ-commissioned pride," swells when we resist the temptation to retaliate with a vengeance, choosing instead to let the living Christ lift us until we rise above that pedestrian, negative resentment reaction and instead offer the healing hand of forgiveness. Take humble pride in this: only the offended can forgive. The guilty cannot extend pardon. By offering reconciliation, we are set apart as the least sinful. We move from the defensive to the offensive. We rise from the role of soldier to the role of statesman. We become compatible instead of combatable.

How does our self-esteem reconcile an apparent contradiction between justice offered and mercy extended? We have two choices. Each will affect our self-esteem. Our first choice can be to yield to a strong sense of justice as we fight back—"I'll hate myself if I do not defend myself. I will hate myself if I do not stand up for the principle involved! My dignity demands that justice be meted out." We can choose this negative reaction, and our wounded pride may have been nursed. But let us not confuse this cheap and emotionally draining sensation with the nobler nourishment of healthy self-esteem which will be our pride and prize when we rise to the lofty level of a forgiving spirit. The life-giving, unpolluted water of self-dignity is not drawn from the well of "righteous indignation" but from the spring of consciousness of my relative innocence—a positive position that gives me the honorable right and dignified authority to offer forgiveness. And then we have a second choice. We can bury resentment and absorb hurt, giving it over to Christ. Obviously, if I'm in a wounded position, I can choose to either forgive or condemn. Actually, this means that I'm in the superior position because *I have a choice.* I'm free to choose what my reaction will be, so I shall choose the reaction that brings me the greatest good. I shall not harbor resentment because it would not fill me with joy. Instead, I shall tender forgiveness and feel good about myself.

A Christ-like spirit of beautiful love comes over our whole personality like an angel of peace when we choose to compliment ourselves as bigger persons by offering this gift of forgiveness. It blesses both the bestower and the receiver. When we forgive others for their assaults on our dignity, our self-esteem rises.

There can be no self-esteem without eliminating resentment and guilt. Both resentment and guilt must be washed away in divine grace before we can really feel good about ourselves. Now let us discover how we can be purged of guilt and be personally forgiven.

How can we receive the forgiveness we need? How can we receive the forgiveness that will save our spirits from the demonic, demolishing, and devastating effect of our guilt?

What is desperately needed is a clear and Christ-like understanding of such classical concepts as 1) sin, 2) salvation, and 3) repentance. If we wish the wonderful delights of mental happiness that come with reconciliation, let us examine these three theological concepts.

1. *Sin.* Reformation theology failed to make clear that the core of sin is a lack of self-esteem. If the goal of salvation is to "glorify God," then the solution must result in restoring self-respect, self-esteem, self-worth, and a noble pride in persons. God is glorified when his children are honored. And the self-denigrating person who by his actions wraps himself in a blanket of shame, or allows a distorted religion to envelop this perceived personality in a contrived blanket of shame, offers no joyous blossom of glory to God, his heavenly Father.

I recall a very sincere young man who came with shame and guilt to confess what he was taught was a horrible sin of "self-abuse." He was wisely committed to preserving his sexual virginity until marriage. But the sexual pressures built up, and to keep from getting promiscuously involved in other persons' lives, he said that he simply relieved the pressures alone. With wet eyes and quivering lips he explained, "I masturbate and feel dirty and guilty as hell."

Years later he reminded me of the words I gave him at the time which helped, "Your real self-abuse is self-mortification. That is far more serious than self-masturbation. The tremendous guilt you pile on yourself may well be the deepest hurt of all."

This is not to say that self-indulgences are always sinless. Rather, it is to say that at the deepest level the heart of sin is found in what it causes us to do to ourselves. The most serious sin is the one that causes me to say, "I am unworthy. I may have no claim to divine sonship if you examine me at my worst." For once a person believes he is an "unworthy sinner," it is doubtful if he can really honestly accept the saving grace God offers in Jesus Christ.

At a deep level, sin is self-rejection with the result that we then reject God's grace, we reject his love, we reject his calling—his dream for our life, and we are incapable of believing in the providential possibilities God has for us. We miss the mark because we fail to achieve what we could and should. We continue to sin, i.e., reflect the lack of faith which results in our ongoing rejection of the potentially God-glorifying opportunities before us. And our lives fail to glorify God.

2. *Salvation.* What does it mean to be saved? It means to be permanently lifted from sin (psychological self-abuse with all of its consequences as seen above) and shame to self-esteem and its God-glorifying human need-meeting, constructive, and creative consequences. To be saved is to know that Christ forgives me and I now dare to believe that I am somebody and I can do something for God and for my fellow human beings. Christianity with its doctrine of salvation is a faith designed by God for the glory of the human being for the greater glory of God.

We are saved from shame to serve with honor. This means that salvation bestows God's glorious gift of a well-understood, well-accepted, deeply appreciated, unmerited and undeserved, highly self-motivating gift of self-esteem. And the result is that we become possibility thinkers—with God all things are now possible; "I can do all things through Christ who strengthens me." As such, we are enabled and motivated to live a life of such good works that we do glorify God with a positive self-image so based on God's unconditional grace that we are deeply, profoundly, personally, inwardly secure. We can be open and honest without any need to wear masks or fear exposure. We don't need to put others down to bolster our faltering human egos. This way I can always feel good living with myself, and I will treat others respectfully, too. I won't have such a weak self-image or malnourished or handicapped ego that I must always have my own way and insist that others always agree with me. Salvation offers a "double blessing of self-esteem." First, I can enjoy the blessing myself, and then I can pass it along to others.

How can God forgive us when we are sinful? How can he save us? The biblical and theological answer is by grace—"God's love in action for people who don't deserve it." (I may not deserve it, but I am worth it, so don't say I am unworthy). In practical terms, here's how it works. God honors us and every human being by giving us the highest, self-esteem-building compliments through the Incarnation, Crucifixion, and Resurrection of Jesus Christ.

By *the incarnation of Jesus Christ God honored the human race*. Negative-thinking theologians delight in pointing out the negative side of that coin, i.e., the Incarnation was the humiliation of Christ. But I choose to emphasize the positive side: The Incarnation was God's glorification of the human being. We bestow a great honor when we call on someone's home! And that is what Christ did when he visited our earth in human form.

While Christ was on earth he remained sinless—he never shamed himself or others. He never called any *person* "a sinner." Rather he reserved his righteous rebuke for those who used their religious authority to generate guilt and caused people to lose their ability to taste and enjoy their right to dignity (Matt. 23).

By remaining sinless, Christ became the historical Ideal Person. This is all-important, for only the innocent can forgive. Only the pure can pardon. When the Ideal One invites us to accept his divine pardon and join him in his high and holy work of building a society where human beings treat each other with dignity, suddenly the offer of pardon, the declaration of credited righteousness on our behalf, the call to meaningful service, all lead us into an existential encounter with such unconditional love and acceptance that we are literally born again. To be accepted by a shameful, horrible person does nothing for our self-esteem. But to be accepted and loved by the noblest of all persons really releases us from a negative self-image! Now we are able to forgive ourselves, and we are motivated to forgive others. We stop putting them down and start building them up!

This means that having been saved, we can serve God and humanity. Having experienced nonjudgmental love, we can pass it on and love others unconditionally.

By his crucifixion Christ has placed God's value upon us. How does Christ's death atone for our sins? How can we say that we are saved by the blood of Christ? In three ways. (1) The Cross of Christ brings vitality to my dignity. If the deepest curse of sin is what it does to our self-esteem, then the atoning power of the Cross is what it does to redeem our discarded self-worth. I know the value of a piece of property only when I have a solid cash offer to buy it—an offer from a person or firm of impeccable integrity. I know the value of my life when I see the price God paid on the cross to save my soul. For the Scriptures say God values us so highly he died for us! (John 3:16). (2) The Cross of Christ makes atonement from guilt possible because *it adds integrity to the positive Gospel.* If Christianity was all smiles and no suffering it would be branded a phony religion. In the Cross of Christ we see the harsh reality of "negativity," "demonic human behavior," "collectivized social evil in institutions" (In this case organized religion was the primary culprit!). We proclaim a religion of good news—with integrity! We recognize horrific forces of demonic negativity potentially infecting persons and institutions. (3) The Cross of Christ adds *morality to divine forgiveness.* For a judge to send every guilty rapist and murderer scot-free under the banner of mercy would turn love into an immoral act. Mercy must be tempered by justice. Negativity must pay its dues. Evil must be punished. So Christ has taken the rap "for our irresponsible negative behavior." He experienced hell—on the cross. For he experienced the loss of glory and total humiliation and shame when he was crucified as a common criminal and hung naked! How they scorned him: "He saved others—himself he cannot save." He experienced total loss of self-esteem that turned hours of shameful exposure into an eternity of hell. Now he can, as my living Lord, forgive me of my sins. His suffering is credited to my personal account. So God cannot punish sins twice over, even as he cannot fail to demand justice. So God is morally able and obligated to offer forgiveness to any person who claims the credit card of Calvary's Cross to cover the guilt of his sinful behavior.

By his resurrection Christ has given us the highest honor—the opportunity to do his work and take his place in the world. Now Christ honors us by commissioning us to be his ambassadors, his statesmen, in the world community. We really are somebodies! He has stepped aside to give us by his grace the honored position of being channels of his healing love. What greater honor could Christ bestow on the human race than to step aside and ask us to become his body (Eph. 5:30); his ambassadors (2 Cor. 5:20); his voice; his hands; his heart; his mind (1 Cor. 2:16).

Christ, then, is our hope of glory.

In his incarnation, Christ has honored the human race.

In his crucifixion, Christ has placed unlimited value on the human soul.

In his resurrection, Christ has passed on to the human race his own glorious ministry. He has "taken early retirement" and given us his joyous work of sharing self-esteem love with every person we meet.

In the courtyard of a quaint little church in a French village there stood a beautiful marble statue of Jesus with his hands outstretched. One day during the World War a bomb struck too close and the statue was dismembered. After the battle was over and the enemy had passed through, the citizens of the village decided to find the pieces of their beloved statue and reconstruct it. While it was no work of art by Michelangelo or Bernini, it was a part of their lives and they loved it. Patiently they gathered the broken pieces and reassembled it. Even the scars on the body added to its beauty. But there was one problem. They were unable to find the hands of the statue. "A

Christ without hands is no Christ at all," someone lamented. "Hands with scars, yes. But what's a Lord without hands? We need a new statue." Then someone else came along with another idea, and it prevailed. A brass plaque was attached at the base of the statue which reads, "I have no hands but your hands."

Some years later, someone saw that inscription and wrote these little lines:

I have no hands but your hands to do my work today.
I have no feet but your feet to lead men on the way.
I have no tongue but your tongue to tell men how I died.
I have no help but your help to bring men to God's side.

By sending his Holy Spirit into our believing and receiving hearts Christ completed the complimenting, converting cycle and circle of self-esteem. Now we are a positively possessed people. We are Holy Spirit-led and Holy Spirit-controlled persons who possess the fruit of the Spirit, ". . . love, joy, peace, patience, kindness, goodness, faithfulness, gentleness, self-control. . . ."

We truly become self-esteeming persons on a Spirit-led campaign to share this gift of self-esteem-generating grace with everyone we meet. Then and only then do we really understand and experience at the deepest, positive level what it means to forgive and be forgiven.

For to be forgiven is not merely a negation of our guilt, rather—it is a positive injection of saving and soaring faith! For when God forgives, he does not merely eliminate our debt, he gives us a new lease on life. He replaces guilt with a new dream and gives us the trust to take hold of it. Possessed by his Holy Spirit we can trust ourselves, we can trust the God who created and redeemed us, and we can trust his dreams. Self-esteem, born in salvation by grace, produces dynamic possibility thinking.

3. *Repentance.* Real repentance is a positive, dynamic and

highly-motivated redirection of life from a guilt-induced fear and its consequent withdrawal from the divine call to a caring, risky trust which promises the hope of glory, for yourself and your heavenly Father, through noble, human-need-filling achievements.

Historical theology has too often failed to interpret repentance as a positive creative force. *Metanoia,* the Greek word for repentance, does not mean self-condemnation, self-denigration, self-abasement. Rather, it means the turning of one's life from sin to the Lordship of Christ. It is a turning from sin, with its rejection of self-esteem as the way to self-fulfillment to sanctification—the way of the Cross, which we shall examine in the next chapter.

Essentially, if Christianity is to succeed in the next millennium, it must cease to be a negative religion and must become positive.

Negative-thinking theologians looked at the doctrine of sin, salvation, and repentance (yes, even the Incarnation, Crucifixion, and, to a degree, the Resurrection) through distorted glasses tinted with a mortification mentality.

Too many prayers of confession of sin and repentance have been destructive to the emotional health of Christians by feeding their sense of nonworth.

If the slate is washed clean of guilt, I am only half forgiven. I am not fully forgiven until I allow God to write his new dream for my life on the blackboard of my mind, and I dare to believe "I am; therefore, I can. I am a child of God. I am somebody. God has a great plan to redeem society. He needs me and wants to use me." These positive affirmations can become commonplace in the church of Christ that is reformed to glorify God by glorifying his children.

The emerging church, reformed according to the needs of self-esteem-starved-souls under the Lordship of Christ and in the grace of God, will help us to affirm the concept that "While God's ideas may seem humanly impossible, he will give us these ideas which will lead to glorious, self-esteem-generating success. I must trust him.

"God has forgiven me for my sins, but too often I have rejected his ideas; I have underrated and berated myself as unworthy and incapable. God promises that by his inspiring possibility thinking—generated by the Holy Spirit—I shall be made capable of achieving something wonderful for him. I can be a beautiful person. I have every reason to start feeling good about myself, and I'm going to have a rich future.

"God's forgiving grace is incomplete until he gives me—and I accept—a new kingdom-building dream and opportunity. And I'll know I am fully forgiven when I'm handed my personal cross, with all of its crucifying challenges."

————Chapter Eight————

Enthusiasm—The Mark of a Healthy Human Being

IF WE KNOW WE are being led into a vital and exciting life filled with new possibilities and dynamic potential, we can be enthusiastic about tomorrow—today! The key to enthusiasm is to know that there is a fulfilling future waiting for us.

Enthusiasm is a positive emotion that deserves our attention. For the alternative too often is cynicism, despair, and depression.

Dr. Bertram Brown, director of the National Institute of Mental Health, has cited depression as the *number one problem* in this country today. "We have to make a frontal attack on the feeling of helplessness that's causing depression in our country today," he stated. "Depression costs the United States of America five billion dollars a year in direct hospital and drug costs. We have no way of calculating how many more multiplied billions of dollars it costs our country in indirect costs such as broken families, alcoholism, drug addiction, and welfare payments to people who have become emotional cripples." Depression is the single most costly emotional illness in the United States of America today.

"Interestingly enough," Dr. Brown continued, "we have

found surprisingly fewer suicides around Christmas time; but as yet, however, we haven't analyzed why."[1] We, of course, know why there are fewer suicides at Christmas time. Suicide is the extreme act of self-rejection. When a person loses all self-love, the will to self-destruct takes over. Christmas is a time of positive therapy because the season has built within it the spirit of spreading self-esteem. Presenting a thoughtful gift is a boost to a person's self-worth. Meanwhile anticipating receiving greetings and well-wishes from others also has a positive effect as far as private and collective self-esteem is concerned.

What's the cure for depression? The positive answer is really very simple: GET ENTHUSIASTIC ABOUT LIFE! Dr. Brown, in his article, speaks to this when he says, "We have to give people success experiences until they realize that their lives are not helpless or hopeless." Of course, a "success" experience is a self-affirming experience. Success stimulates and sustains our self-esteem. Our emerging self-esteem, in turn, generates a healthy enthusiasm.

Now, if depression can be cured by inspiring people to be enthusiastic, how do we go about making that happen? This is achieved by giving them encouragement, motivation, and education which can increase the quantity and quality of their success experiences. Here's how the enthusiasm-generating process works. Self-esteem will give rise to a new dream ("I am," therefore, "I can"). The dream holds great possibilities for further self-esteem-producing successes, and enthusiasm evolves correspondingly.

Now comes the danger. There is a price tag connected to every dream. The higher the honor, the higher the cost. There is no crown without a cross. There is no success without sacrifice. And the refusal to pay the price that success demands is the number one reason for failure. Here, then, is a major cause of the spreading epidemic of that depression which follows failure. For when we reject the price, we enter the withdrawal stage, and in emotional retreat we sense the withering of enthusiasm-generating hopes, and a depression begins to fill the vacuum. There is no resurrection without death; no success without sacrifice; no gain without pain, no accomplishment without commitment, and no commitment without conflict. For there is no commitment without involvement; there is no involvement without self-denial; and there is no self-denial without personal sacrifice. So the process adds up to this fact: every act of sincere sacrifice will generate self-esteem whether I succeed or fail. ("I did what I had to do. I'm able to live with myself without shame! So the pathway to enthusiasm is the pathway of self-sacrifice.")

This being so, what then is the danger we can anticipate? The danger will be that we are tempted to think we can somehow avoid risky and costly commitments.

So what do we need to pray now in order to keep our enthusiasm going, growing, and glowing?: "Lead us not into temptation." This could be the most important chapter in the book; it is the crucial step in the process of getting to feel really good about ourselves.

Let's summarize the substance of a theology of self-esteem and convert the theological principles into practical affirmation.

Step One: *I overcome my inferiority.* I discover God as Father. "Our Father who is in heaven."

Step Two: *I overcome my discouragement.* I believe God is building a society of redeemed, redeeming persons and he needs me. "Your kingdom come, your will be done."

Step Three: *I am assured of success.* God will inspire me with self-affirming ideas that can lead me to fulfill his will. "Give us this day our daily bread."

Step Four: *I am established in a positive relationship with*

God, and my fellow human brothers and sisters. Forgiveness and faith are mine. "Forgive us our debts as we forgive our debtors."

Step Five: *I am confronted with the cost of discipleship.* The price of success; the pains and perils of achievement now come to mind. "And lead us not into temptation. . . ."

I shall now be faced with the ultimate temptation—the temptation to reject God's plan for my life, for the price will be high. The proclamation of self-esteem and possibility thinking, then, is a *positive proclamation* of a positive theology of the Cross. First, no one will succeed without self-sacrifice. And *when* we achieve success, we inherit a whole new set of challenges. Success may eliminate some problems, but it produces new and different problems.

The promise of success then is not the promise of comfort and ease. Quite the contrary. There is no success without service, and service means involvement in someone else's wants, needs, hurts, and desires. Real success demands the sacrificial role, which by its nature calls for unselfishness and an attitude of sacrificial commitment. Can this really be the pathway to depression-dispelling enthusiasm? Yes! It was for our Lord, "Who for the joy that was set before him endured the cross" (Heb. 12:2). This same promise of and pathway to joy was offered to his disciples when Christ prayed before his death, ". . . that they may have my joy fulfilled in themselves" (John 17:13).

If we want to be enthusiastic, really enthusiastic, it's very simple. Enthusiasm comes when we set for ourselves exciting and challenging goals. Of course, every time we set a new goal, we generate a new set of tensions. Will I win or lose? Will I be proud in success? Or ashamed in failure? Every time we set a new goal, we create a whole new class of conflicts. We must remember that not everyone will agree with us, and we may have to part company with friends and partners. When we make commitments to a God-inspired dream and give it all we've got, that produces enthusiasm. But when we hold ourselves back and are not totally committed, we create an emotional blockage which restricts the flow of natural, godly enthusiasm.

There's another dimension that we must accept. No self-esteem-feeding, enthusiasm-generating, depression-dispelling, honor-bestowing success, will ever be achieved unless it is conceived in love. And the definition for this kind of possibility-thinking-love is found in this ten-word sentence: "Love is my decision to make your problem my problem." That is precisely what God did for you and me when Christ was crucified. So we see that:

1) The Cross of Christ is described as an act of supreme divine love (John 3:16).

2) We are saved by faith made possible through Christ's death (John 3:16).

3) The Cross of Christ was an act of divine love. For God was making our human problem his problem. Our problem was and is a lack of self-worth. The Cross is God's solution to humanity's shame: For the Cross of Christ is God's price tag of value on the lowliest person. "For God so loved the *world* that he gave his only Son, that *whoever* believes in him should not perish but have eternal life" (John 3:16). How did the Cross solve the problem of humanity's humiliation? God was demonstrating the infinite value of every and any person. God was telling the world that he would stop at nothing to eliminate guilt and shame from any soul.

Therefore, to choose success as a goal is to choose the Cross as the Way! To choose failure or to accept failure or to condone and write apologies for failure is an act of defensive rationalization. Too often it is an attempt to rescue a wounded self-worth from the terrible assaults a "failure-image" bestows on a person or an institution. In the process we may become advocates for persons who were actually unwilling to bear the Cross God had in store for them.

Let us retrace our Lord's Prayer pathway to self-esteem.

Step One: "Our Father . . . in heaven . . ." I'm reconciled to my Father. I'm a prince of heaven.

Step Two: "Thy kingdom come, thy will be done . . ." God has saved me to call me into his service of love.

Step Three: "Give us this day our daily bread . . ." God will not let me fail in his service. He shall supply my need.

Step Four: "Forgive us our debts, as we forgive . . ." My guilt for past and present and future failures is wiped out. I am forgiven. My self-esteem is conceived and born in divine grace.

Now we must understand that forgiveness is not only the erasing of guilt for past sins. A far more positive meaning must be placed on forgiveness. After God forgives, he proceeds to trust us by entrusting us with a daring, divine dream.

We may now expect to be offered a dangerous mission, and we will need to pray: "Lead me not into temptation." And this gives rise to two questions:

1) What is the ultimate temptation we need to be protected from?

2) How can God answer this prayer?

First, I believe that our ultimate temptation as self-respecting members of God's kingdom will be to reject the Cross we are called to carry.

Second, I am convinced that God's prescription to preserve us from temptation is positive and not negative. He will cause us to be so enthusiastic about the divine dream that we will disregard the cost and make the commitment.

And in making that commitment we accept the pain of the problems, and we are sustained against the pressures by God's mercy until the battle is won, conflicts are resolved, injustice is corrected, criticism is replaced by sincere compliments, the project is accomplished, the achievement is now tied up in a ribbon, the new church building is dedicated, the hospital is finished, the cure is finally discovered.

Tremendous human energy is needed to walk God's walk, work God's work, fulfill God's will, and complete his dream for our self-esteem. Powerful motivation is needed to launch forth and sustain, without surrender, the goal of the God-ordained mission he has for every person. So, unless there is a steady source of enthusiasm, defeat is certain.

What then should we hope for in answer to the prayer, "Lead us not into temptation"? If we are coming from the historical position of negative Christianity we are really saying, "Oh God, keep me from committing conspicuous immoral sins." But of itself, this is vacuous, i.e., nonconstructive. I plead for the deeper meaning. God calls us to a positive plan. We all know people who do not lie, kill, steal, commit adultery, yet they live a life of ease, comfort, and noninvolvement. They appear to be kind and gentle, and we are tempted to judge them to be "loving people." But real love is sacrificial commitment. Until these "good people" set God-glorifying goals, they are making no potentially creative and constructive commitments. If they take no daring risk in mission, they're good—but good for what?

The ultimate temptation is to reject the Cross which God's call always includes. This means that we must constantly pray that God will motivate us to see and seize his honorable goals for our life. Then we must lay a spiritual siege around his glorious possibility to protect it from the temptation to surrender our God-given dreams to the enemy of ease and comfort.

No sentence of our Lord puts the issue before us more clearly than these words, "If any man would come after me, let him deny himself and take up his cross and follow me" (Matt. 16:24). But to understand the full implications of these words we must look carefully at the demands of discipleship that those who are God's dreamers must face if they are to really stay on the self-esteem cycle.

Lead us not into the temptation to avoid self-denial. To understand what this sentence means we need to know what is meant by self-denial. In the first place it is not self-denigration. Self-denial does not mean that God calls us to humiliation. He is not glorified by our self-debasement with the attitude that "I am nothing," "I am unworthy," "I am a worthless sinner." Such attitudes are dangerous distortions and destructive misinterpretations of scattered Bible verses grossly misread by negative-thinking Bible readers who project their own negative self-image onto the pages of Holy Scripture. There can be no defense for any interpretation of Scripture which would inspire persons to think less of themselves than God thinks of them. We can all understand how a low self-image will result in low achievement.

Surely Christ's call to self-denial does not mean self-flagellation. Roman Catholic and Reformed theology has not adequately demanded a halt to a poisonous mortification mood and message that still thrives in certain Christian literature. Not a few congregations have listened to scolding sermons from an angry pulpit. Pious congregants sit and absorb the verbal punishment like a meek child being spanked by a stern Father. And then upon leaving the church they are heard to praise the emotional whipping, "What a great sermon."

How can they feel positive about such a negative experience? They rationalize, consciously or subconsciously, that, "If I accept a low enough image of myself and if I accept the punishment I deserve because of my failures and sins, then I shall be personally atoning for my sins and I'll be cleansed. I'll feel good, and can accept myself again." Self-flagellation is a sad and subtle attempt to earn salvation by works!

Are we to believe that self-denial means the denial of personal pleasure, desire, fulfillment, prosperity? For too long religious leaders have suggested this with tragic results. Many marriages have been broken because of a negative view of sex within marriage. Untold numbers of Christians have remained on a poverty level because the pursuit of money and wealth was always proclaimed to be a sinful and materialistic value in modern American culture. And it is a strange paradox that the same voices that condemn money as a legitimate Christian value cry out against poverty, even as they condemn motivators who would inspire persons to strive to achieve financial independence.

Such thinking is a tragic distortion of truth. To fail to inspire persons to strive for financial security and ultimate financial independence leaves them vulnerable to any ambitious, politically power-hungry manipulator. After all, if I'm not encouraged to save and invest wisely my acquired money, I will be forever *dependent* on the state—on society—for the health, education, and welfare of myself and my family. The more dependent I am the less sense of freedom to be creative, the less self-esteem I can experience, the less joy of giving I can know. The poor cannot help the poor.

In reality, the positive self-esteem-generating solution to the poverty problem in our world today is the creation and expansion of opportunities for all persons to acquire money and invest their private dollars successfully (i.e., projects, enterprises, and corporations organized to create job opportunities and serve humanity).

By self-denial Christ does not mean the rejection of that positive emotion we call self-esteem—the joy of experiencing my self-worth—the joy of discovering my roots, and hence my spiritual identity—the joy of discovering my inheritance, my legacy, as a child of God—the joy of discovering my latent talent and possibilities to become a creative, redemptive, helpful, human being in society—the joy of discovering that I can cease to be a dependent burden on others and instead become independent enough to be free to lift someone else's burden. Surely to encourage us to suppress these positive emotions in the name of "Christian self-denial" is oppressive and negative.

By self-denial we cannot accept that Christ is calling us to a dishonest and demeaning humility. I have no doubt that *millions,* yes, multiplied millions of God-given, self-esteem-generating dreams and ideas have been sent by God's Holy Spirit into Christian minds who forthrightly rejected them—for one *reason* . . . the idea immediately promised ego fulfillment. Poor misguided, sincere Christian souls, sensing the birth of noble self-esteem as they imagine the development of this dream, told themselves, "This must be pride. It must be my will, and that means it cannot be God's will." God's biggest problem is to motivate us to accept his divine dreams even if they hold the prospect of ego-fulfillment. God's dreams always hold the promise of self-esteem satisfaction. We need not, however, fear that we shall be "guilty of going off on an ego trip" if we pursue those divine ideas that hint at the possibility cf some personal glory along the way. For there will be a cross before we gain the crown. And *the cross will sanctify the ego trip!*

So often, out of an innocent, child-like, sincere Christian faith and the pursuit of a beautiful humility, God's great ideas are rejected. Likewise many successful Christians suffer from the guilt that arises with the "pride of achievement." They succeed only to become lonely achievers. What is worse, the loneliness of failure or the loneliness of success? If we are mentally healthy we will feel a noble, honorable, and healthy pride when a costly accomplishment is finally realized. Then where can we find someone with whom we can share in our rejoicing? (They'll think I'm boastful!) If our perception of modesty conflicts with our honesty, let us tell the truth—let us praise God for our success and praise him for our prosperity! Then let us enjoy the victory! Surely self-denial does not mean the joy of self-esteem that is God's blessing on that disciple who enjoys success after making great sacrifices.

So what is the real Christ-call to self-denial? It is a willingness to be involved in the spiritual and social solutions in society. But only the inwardly secure, self-respecting, self-accepting person can be trusted to enter the vulnerable arena of social involvement. Persons with a positive self-image will become positively prophetic, while the ego-starving person becomes "negatively prophetic." What is the difference between the two? It's the difference between confrontation and construction—between generating a social climate of polarization versus creating a community where creative and mutually respectful dialogue can happen.

Self-affirmation then is the pathway to self-denial. "I am a worthy person. I have something to give, therefore, I can succeed in service, and I dare to volunteer." This means there will be no self-denial without strong self-esteem. And self-denial is the daring commitment of your name, your reputation, your integrity, your ego, on the altar of God's call to service. Mark this, it is important: The greatest cross any person can carry is to risk sacrificing his or her ego by risking the embarrassment of a public failure in the pursuit of some noble, honorable, God-inspired dream. That is *positive self-denial.* It is denying your ego the selfish protection from a possible humiliating failure that might occur if you tried to carry out the divine idea.

No one is more vulnerable than the person who makes a public commitment before he or she can be assured of success. At such times we must be prepared to suffer an ego blowout at high speed in heavy traffic. For in giving leadership to taking an idea and selling it to those whose approval is necessary, we risk criticism and mockery. So fear of a possible failure is enough to stop many a person from pursuing a great, God-given idea (which is to say we are unwilling to run the risk of having our proper pride crucified on the altar of public criticism). *That fear of public rejection, I submit, is the ultimate selfishness.* This retreat from the divine call is the exact opposite of the self-denial Christ's call to discipleship demands. *Christ's call to self-denial, after all, is always a call to a commitment to do something creative and constructive.*

The classical interpretation of this teaching of Christ on "bearing our cross" desperately needs reformation. In view of this need, let us look now at what "bearing our cross" really means. It is not a call to self-pity. Again and again a wounded life, injured in body or heart, seeks a neurotic self-pitying refuge around this misinterpreted command of Christ.

"Bearing the cross" is not a call to indulge in a persecution complex. Criticism, condemnation, or rejection cannot be authentic cross-bearing unless it is the price we pay to launch and carry out our God-given dream.

In addition we cannot accept the "cross-bearing" principle as being positively fulfilled by a crusader complex. Too often well-intentioned reformers of social or spiritual ills have chosen the provocative, inflammatory, polarization-producing, confrontation approach instead of the patient-mind-changing, prejudice-reducing, fear-dissolving, dialogue approach. Then, when verbal or physical violence resulted, the crusaders, bleeding and battered, proudly declared that they had faithfully fulfilled their call to carry their cross. Granted there have been times in history when crusaders may have been successful, the crusade strategy remains a dangerous *style* for social correction. Certainly, this should be the exception—not the normal positive intent in the mind of Christ when he called for the "bearing of one's cross."

Let us look now at the positive side of the question. What then is the real call to the carrying of one's cross? What is the cross we must bear? The cross Christ calls us to bear will be offered as a dream, an idea. It is not imposed; we must *choose* to fully accept it. It will appear as an inspiring idea that would incarnate itself in a form of ministry that helps self-esteem-impoverished persons to discover their self-worth through salvation and subsequent social service in our Savior's name. My cross, your cross will be an opportunity. And every opportunity seized will be a seedbed of new problems that will tax us severely.

The cross will be a glorious possibility, a divine call to mission and service. It will be a call to commitment. We will have "taken up our cross" when we have said, "Here am I, Lord, use me." The cross? It will be a call to take a chance. Every act of faith is a call to sacrifice. When we make the decision to try, while there still remain unresolved obstacles and unsolved problems, then we are moving and living by what the Bible calls FAITH. And faith means that we sacrifice the safety and security of noninvolvement. Such decision-making faith is the automatic lifting to one's shoulders of the cross Christ asks us to bear. And with all of this, something good will emerge which will glorify God because we are paying the price. Then, "cross bearing" becomes a positive act, not a negative reaction.

Naturally the fear of rejection, the possibility of a public humiliating failure, is a terrible threat to the ego. It will call for a tremendous burst of divinely inspired enthusiasm to resist the temptation to play it safe, take care, and reject the Cross. "Lord, lead us not into temptation."

The rejection of the Cross was the temptation Christ faced in the Garden of Gethsemane. Was he, too, not tempted to choose the easy failure that comes from rejecting the Cross instead of choosing the glorious success that would be his if he accepted the cross? But it was in his dying that his words, "I, if I be lifted up from the earth, will draw all men unto me" (John 12:32, KJV), became a reality.

So the proclamation of possibility thinking is the positive proclamation of the Cross!

We can begin to see the positive enthusiasm-generating, depression-dispelling power on this command of Christ, "If anyone would come after me, he must deny himself and take up his cross and follow me" (Matt. 16:24, NIV).

". . . And follow me"? What does that mean? It means daring to dream a great dream!

Divine dreams are the tap roots of enthusiasm. So, we are called to join God's kingdom. You and I are called to be modern disciples of Jesus. We are called to think of the possibilities God has for us. We are called to deny ourselves, take up our cross, and follow him.

Christ was the world's greatest possibility thinker. Do we dare to follow him? He was enthusiastic about the success potential of his enterprise! Do we dare dream dreams? We must if we are to fulfill Christ's words, "Go ye into all the world, and preach the gospel to every creature" (Mark 16:15, KJV).

We must prayerfully be spared from the temptation to follow a cynical, suspicious, insecure world. "Wide is the gate and broad is the way that leads to destruction, and there are many who go in through it." Then Jesus went on to say, "Because narrow is the gate and difficult is the way which leads to life, and there are few who find it" (Matt. 7:13–14, NKJV).

Yes, the majority of persons are impossibility thinkers. They are the dream smashers, the project torpedo-ers, the cross-evaders, enthusiasm-deflators, depression-spreaders. May God deliver us from them. And may he lead us to follow Christ, the Possibility Thinker.

Perhaps no portion of the Bible summarizes this chapter's lesson more beautifully than the fifteenth chapter of the Gospel of John. Here we discover that:

1. God chooses us to serve his purpose. "You did not choose me, but I chose you." Our self-esteem is rooted in our divine call. God's dream for our life and work gives purpose and pride to our life. Our role is clear; we are to be the branches of Christ's love in the world, "I am the vine, you are the branches."

2. God's plan and purpose calls for us to succeed and not to fail. "I am the vine, you are the branches. He who abides in me . . . bears much fruit." Here then is our definition of success. To succeed is to "bear fruit," i.e., to be productive. In a sentence: success is that happy and humble feeling of pride and self-esteem we feel when we have helped someone else along life's way. We must, therefore, never stop believing in success. For when we succeed, all of society will benefit—we can't possibly succeed without helping a lot of people along the way. And if we fail, who really fails? Everyone is hurt when we fail to "bear fruit." The people who could have been helped if we had succeeded are left hurting and hungry. But failure weakens us, emotionally and perhaps financially, too. Surely it limits our power to be helpful. For, success might be seen as a study in power—how to get it; how to keep it; how to restrain it; how not to abuse it; how to use it; how to share it!

3. There will be no success without a cross: "The world

will hate you—even as they have hated me." Ambitious possibility thinkers are a threat to the less motivated!

4. God is glorified when we succeed. "By this my Father is glorified, that you bear much fruit" (John 15:8). How does success, as we define it, glorify God? The fruitful person is self-affirmed in his success experience. As a result, he is enthusiastic. He is free from the tensions and hangups that afflict the insecurity-plagued nonachievers. As a result, the self-esteem generates greater enthusiasm (*en Theos,* "in-God," i.e., a branch that is abiding in the vine!). The greater enthusiasm releases greater energy and greater self-confidence to attempt greater works for God. "And you shall bear more fruit." The peak experience (self-affirming success experience) produces a peek experience (a new vision of greater things that I can do for him!).

There will be no success without self-denial and cross-bearing. But we gain assurance as we remember the words of Jesus, "If the world hates you, keep in mind that it hated me first" (John 15:18, NIV). May God hear and answer our prayer and protect us from the temptation to seek success without the cross.

---------- Chapter Nine ----------

Freedom from Fear Is
Freedom to Love

"DELIVER US FROM evil." Deliver us from what? "Evil!"

Interesting. We are not taught by our Lord to ask God to deliver us from grief or pain or tears or sorrow or even from the Devil himself.

But Jesus did tell us to pray for deliverance from evil. What might that be? The Devil, you say? But if that were so, why didn't Christ name him? Could it be that Jesus hopes we would understand what he knew—the Devil whom Christ encountered personally was and still is finite, not infinite. If we interpret literally the Scripture passages that trace the origin of this mastermind behind organized evil, we are led to believe that Satan was a fallen angel. And angels, like humans, are finite, i.e., they can only be in one place at a time. It is unlikely that those of us who live on planet earth will ever encounter the Devil personally. But we are all certainly subject to his evil influence in the world. There is good news, though; Scripture declares that the power of Satan has been destroyed by the death and resurrection of Jesus Christ (Heb. 2:14, 15).

I find the frequent references to Satan by many sincere Christians, and the extraordinary tributes given him, to be repugnant. We so often hear someone say, "The Devil made me do it." Really? We should not be so quick to give the Devil credit for more activities than he deserves. The Devil would love to get credit for any success he can claim. The last thing a Christian should do is to honor Satan by giving him what he wants—public credit for evil.

Let us instead honor Christ by affirming his positive control over our lives, thereby making the power of the Devil impotent and ineffective. Remember, "He who is in you is greater than he who is in the world" (1 John 4:4).

The Devil is clever. There is nothing he'd like more than to see us try to shift the responsibility for our sins neatly onto him. That way he would get the credit, honor, or glory for our sins. By copping out on our personal accountability, we avoid the real act of constructive repentence.

What then does Christ mean, "Deliver us from evil"? If Scripture must interpret Scripture, then we can approach the word *evil* the way we peel an onion. The outer layers are labeled murder, rape, exploitation, oppression, etc. Then as we continue to peel away more layers, we come to contributing sins like covetousness, greed, and jealousy. On still deeper levels, closer to the center, we find insecurity and inferiority. Next comes fear, also called lack of trust, because fear is the precise opposite of trust. Peel this layer away and you find the final nucleus—a negative self-image, a lack of self-esteem.

I am indebted to Dr. Gerald Jampolsky, a guest on our "Hour of Power," for helping me to see what is not only great psychology, but is profound theology. Obviously, there can be no conflict in truth—when psychology is "right on" and theology is "right on," there will be harmony and both shall be led to higher levels of enlightenment. "The two basic emotions," Dr. Jampolsky said, "are love and fear." Fear, then, is another word for lack of love, lack of self-love, i.e., low self-esteem.

Fear is the projection of the deeper emotion called insecurity, and insecurity is a reflection of a lack of self-confidence. And if we trace the roots of an inadequate self-confidence, we find a person with a very negative self-image. Then, we're right back where we started—the whole ultimate issue of self-esteem. So, persons with a low self-esteem are prone to fear.

When we pray, "Deliver us from evil," we are trusting to be delivered from fear and its violent effects in our lives, and from the sources and stimuli that give birth to our fears. We are also praying that we will be possessed by such a positive faith and love that we shall be immune to the negative, fear-generating, evil forces. And we are praying that we will be positive personalities that shall never cause fear to rise in the lives of others. Instead, our mission will be to spread self-esteem-producing love, "Perfect love casts out fear" (1 John 4:18). We shall be partners with God and participants in his kingdom of self-esteem by becoming a healing influence as we inspire courage in others. The slogan, "God loves you and so do I," will be deep therapy for troubled, insecure, non-self-affirming, fearful souls.

The evil, active force of fear can be intensely destructive in our lives and in society. This is vividly illustrated in such evils as racial prejudice and religious conflict.

What is racial prejudice? Is it hate, or is it the subtle, yet deep-seated fear one race has of another? Then, too, what is behind so much of the religious conflict we find in our world? Is it a form of hatred and prejudice and bigotry? Or is that suggestion too simplistic? On the other hand, if we see fear as lack of self-esteem or an impoverished self-love as one side of a coin and a deep inner hostility and anger as the other, then we can begin to understand the insanities that tear us apart and create suspicion and hostility—and, ultimately verbal violence.

With perceptive insight, Paul Tournier, the brilliant Swiss psychiatrist writes in his book entitled *The Violence*

Within: "Every human being has the potential for violence erupting from within himself." It is this fact that has long made me nervous and uncomfortable with the popular strategy of confrontation advocated by many religious leaders as the proper approach to addressing a difference of opinion and grievance.

I am a firm believer that we should never attack any problem until we can do it with a positive plan, with a creative idea, with a noninflammatory dream. We need constantly to be reminded that while the persons with whom we are dealing may appear on the surface to be hateful, in reality, they are afraid . . . they are fearful and feel threatened. Under these circumstances a nonpositive and uncreative approach can so easily erupt into verbal violence, and this is always dangerous and often destructive. It is only as we develop a positive approach to differences and problems that we can be hopeful our actions will introduce an inspiring solution. Then we will avoid fanning the flames of conflict.

The destructive evil force of fear can be passive as well as active. Not only can it provoke hatred and violence, destroying the possibility of the unity in the family of God, but fear's silent sting of death on God's positive projects, in the minds of his possibility-thinking people, is equally destructive. Fear erodes feelings of self-worth. Fear feeds that "I can't cope" syndrome. It nourishes the "I can't do it" complex. Fear encourages the "let's quit" mood. Fear is the eternal demon that whispers poison into the lofty dreamer's mind: "It won't work. It's not worth it. You'll fail and become the laughing stock of everyone."

Fear is the ultimate devil that keeps the lonely, the unhappy, the unloved, the anxiety-prone, the lost sinners, from even listening to the gospel! Why would the hungry refrain from food? They will, if they fear being bitten by the hand that feeds them. It is this attitude that explains why many churches are empty; why the gospel of Christ is unheeded or rejected by millions. Fear is the real reason humanity rejects the unconditional saving grace of God.

Why? We feel too unworthy to accept unearned, unmerited forgiveness and pardon. And we are fearful of a holy God who, because he is holy, could not possibly pardon us. So, our fear turns into doubt, deference, dishonesty, and rebellion.

Now, let's look at the sources and stimuli of fear. We know that it doesn't come from God because in 2 Timothy we read, "For God hath not given us the spirit of fear; but of power, and of love, and of sound mind" (2 Tim. 1:7, KJV). If the spirit of fear does not come from God, where does it come from?

First, it comes from within ourselves. Every time we verbalize or mentally entertain a self-depreciating, self-debasing, self-esteem-assaulting, self-dignity-polluting thought, we are planting the seeds of fear or we are fertilizing the soil of the mind to welcome and nourish the seeds of fear and self-doubt which come too naturally and too easily.

If we allow ourselves to live the undisciplined life of the careless disciple, casually allowing negative thoughts entrance, residence, and nourishment in our minds, then we are our own worst enemy. But if we have accepted God's saving grace and walk in an affirmative path of prayer, we can be delivered from inner fear.

Second, religion itself has too often been a source of fear. Not a few religious movements and institutions, Christianity not excepted, have manipulated guilty, insecure persons by feeding them ideas that would directly generate fear, lack of self-worth, guilt, and anxiety about approaching God.

Jesus never called a *person* a sinner. He vented his sternest rebuke upon whom? The harlot? No. Jesus told her, "Your sins are forgiven, go and sin no more." Was it the secular materialists caught up in their success-oriented culture? No. "Follow me," Jesus said to them, "and I will make you fishers of men." Then who were the objects of Christ's righteous rebukes? And why? They were the well-esteemed, well-established, leaders and lords of the religious institutions of their day. Why them? What did they do that was so evil? Nothing is more evil then the evil that parades under the banner of goodness: "The Devil comes as an angel of light" (2 Cor. 11:14, my translation). Claiming to represent God with the self-anointed authority to speak the Word of God, these Pharisees and members of the religious courts established a set of regulations that were impossible to fulfill and were certain to generate continual guilt. The fear of punishment, the fear of divine rejection, the false sense of guilt, the lack of self-worth, were all propagated in the name of religion. If the Jewish establishment was guilty of that in Christ's day, and if Luther found the Roman Catholic Church guilty in his day, I find the Protestant church far from innocent in our history.

The gospel message is not only faulty, but potentially dangerous if it has to put a person down before it attempts to lift him up. I protest all proclamations of portended Christian messages that *attack the dignity of the person* of a sinner while attacking the sin.

Historical Calvinist theology has failed to make a distinction between "Adam's Sin" and "Original Sin." Adam was created without sin. He had a choice to continue sinless or to sin. He chose to rebel. But his rebellion should not be charged to his children and his children's children.

Adam's descendants were born detached from God, outside of the Garden of Eden where he had cowered in guilt-induced fear. Every person is born "nontrusting" according to Erik Erikson's concept (i.e., lack of self-love or self-esteem, i.e., fearful, lacking in love). Here then is a scientific, scriptural doctrine of original sin. This principle is illustrated by the fact that nurses who care for babies born prematurely in the hospital are instructed to talk to them and stroke them lovingly. This practice grows out of an awareness on the part of medical people that the newborn child comes into the world with feelings of insecurity.

But, tragically, all too often, the church seems insensitive to the basically fearful nature of the nonredeemed human being and contributes to his or her fears by withholding the "stroking" that is so desperately needed. How, then, are we to approach the "unsaved," the naturally insecure, fearful, nontrusting, non-self-loving, non-self-esteeming person who is born with feelings of insecurity and is still living in a jungle of fears? It certainly is not by shouting loud and angry-sounding words at them from the pulpit or by radio and television!

I recall so well when I was visiting in New Guinea that I said I wanted to meet members of a certain tribe who were supposed to be the most primitive persons living today. A guide took me deep into the jungle, and when we arrived at a certain clearing, he stopped and said, "They're all around us, not twelve feet away. They see you, Dr. Schuller. Just smile and hold out your hands with a mirror and some gum. They're fearful, but I think they will come out when they see your smile and what you have in your hands." Slowly, fearfully, they came out and accepted what I had to offer.

This is a beautiful illustration for us of just how we can be God's agents today in presenting his final solution to people for complete deliverance from fear. And what is that final solution? It is salvation through Jesus Christ!

Salvation. What is it? The answer comes to us through some beautifully written words in the forty-third chapter of Isaiah: "Fear not, for when you go through the waters, they will not overflow you. When you go through the fire, it will not consume you, for I am your God. I have redeemed you. I have called you by my name. You are mine. I will be with you" (my translation). The salvation promised in these words offers deliverance from the fear of being an evil person, of being possessed by evil thoughts. To be saved is to be protected from that evil. Salvation is God's final answer to our prayer, "Deliver us from evil." God saves us and comes into our lives through Jesus Christ. Then we can say with the psalmist, "The Lord is my shepherd . . . I will fear no evil" (Ps. 23).

If a spark falls on water, nothing happens. If a spark falls on ice, nothing happens. If a spark falls on asphalt or glass or marble, nothing happens. But if a spark falls on a powder keg, there's a tremendous explosion. Negative and evil thoughts bombard our lives like sparks, and the results are explosive and devastating. But when we are saved and Christ comes into our lives, then when the sparks of temptation or the potential for evil strike our hearts, it will be as if they had fallen on water.

The good news is that God has promised us that any person who wants salvation can have it. And when that happens, Jesus Christ will come into our lives and make a permanent alteration that will irreversibly, divinely transform our deepest character so that we shall never live a life of self-denigration which leads to decadence and depravity. Rather, our life will reflect beauty, glory, honor, and dignity. Christ within us will help develop our innermost potential for good in such a way that, through the pursuit of our God-given possibilities, we will become the person he wants us to be. Again, there is a superb amplification of this thought in a line from Cardinal Karol Wojytla's (Pope John Paul II) writings, "the glory of God is living man; the glory of God is man alive. And God also leads man to glory." When we are so busy doing what Christ wants us to do, we are saved from being distracted and destroyed by the potential for evil which surrounds us. That is the positive outlook on sin and evil! And in this way possibility thinking becomes a positive, preventative theology that inspires our involvement in God-inspired projects. Self-esteem becomes an emotionally nutritional shield against sin.

We are saved from evil when we are saved from shame to self-esteem for service. Now our life has real worth.

Twenty-four years ago, I accepted a call to begin a church in Garden Grove, California. Before we knew it, we were led into a dream of a walk-in, drive-in church so people in their cars could worship with those who were on the inside. But we had problems fulfilling our dream of erecting a beautiful building to the glory of God that would be surrounded by water, trees, birds, and flowers. I didn't have the money to make this dream come true, and I was afraid I would fail. "Oh God," I thought to myself, "what'll I do?" I was haunted by the fear that my life would be a shame to God and a shame to my family. The fear of failure was to haunt me for two years, like a trip in hell The fear of failure was an extreme form of self-doubt, lack of trust, a negative self-image, and an inadequate self-esteem. The destructive evil forces that expressed themselves in a variety of anxieties and negative emotions were a "hell" of an experience.

One night I prayed, "Dear Jesus Christ, if you're alive, and I can't even prove you are, I pray that you'll reach into my mind and take out this horrible fear. Save me." At that very moment I felt a pressure in my head as if a finger had gone down into the innermost recesses of my mind. Then I felt the "invisible finger" withdraw and a load of poisonous fear was drained from my mind, and I was at peace. I have never since been afraid of anything or anyone. I have my times of apprehension, but that's different from fear.

If we will pray, "God, deliver me from evil. God, move deep into my life so that I may know I have been saved from the potential of ever becoming an evil, destructive, negative person. Come into my life, Christ, that I may be your beautiful person." He will redeem us. We will experience salvation. When he saves us, we're saved from evil and we're saved TO beauty! We are now free to love, and we dare to risk rejection because our self-esteem is rooted in a relationship with Christ that transcends all other affectional relationships and will make all human divorces or alienations bearable. We have truly been SAVED! We belong to God. He knows our name, and our prayer, "Deliver us from evil," has been answered for all time.

Chapter Ten

Human Dignity in the Divine Enterprise

THE CLOSING MOVEMENT of the Lord's Prayer reads,
". . . For yours is the kingdom and the power and the
glory forever. Amen." In this sweeping, soaring summary
we are offered the answers to the three most important
questions facing the church and the entire human race.

Question one: What in the world is God trying to do?

Answer: He's building his kingdom: "For yours is the
kingdom."

Question two: How in the world does God hope to
succeed?

Answer: By his power: "For yours is the power."

Question three: Why in the world does God bother about
it?

Answer: For his glory. "For yours is the glory forever."

What hope this holds for a stress-filled, self-esteem-impoverished, sinful humanity! We are told that we can become a member of a compassionate caring community, the
kingdom of God. To succeed without having someone to
share the joys of success is a hollow, lonely, desolate experience. The person who has been saved from shame to
self-esteem now desperately needs to give out the love he
or she has taken in. At the same time the community is

needed to sustain and support our new-found faith. We are offered the delights and the disciplines of a divine community by becoming a part of God's kingdom.

Let us look more closely at the three questions.

If there is a God, what in the world is He trying to do? Of course, the question must begin with an "if," for our faith is just that—faith! Faith is a commitment to an unprovable assumption. The "bottom line" of all questions is: "Is there an intelligent, intervening God?" There are three possible answers to this question. 1) There is no God. Call me an atheist; 2) I won't say; I can't be sure. Call me an agnostic. 3) There is a God. Call me a theist.

Can we be positively certain that any one of these answers is correct? The answer is No! Both the atheist and theist are making a commitment of faith. The atheist believes in nothing. The theist believes in something. But both are making a commitment to an unprovable assumption.

If we cannot be certain that any one of these answers is correct, we must then ask: Can we be positive that any one or more of these answers is certainly wrong? Can we eliminate any one of the three choices as we take the ultimate multiple choice test of our lives? The answer is yes.

Choice two is surely not right. Indecision is a decision, and in this test the agnostic cannot be right. Either there is or there is not an intelligent, involved, universal, eternal God. This leaves us with only one of two choices—to believe there is a God or to choose to believe there is no God.

"Why do you believe in God?" I have often been asked. My answer takes the form of three "I believe" statements.

I believe in God because for me it is intellectually incomprehensible to assume that the orderly universe with all of its known and unknown life forces and spaces, occurred without any creative thought.

I believe in God because I can honestly say without an ounce of reservation that I know I am a better person as a result of my faith in him. And I believe I would hold to the faith even if there were overwhelming evidence pointing to a dark, black, mindless nothingness in the origin of life in the universe. I just cannot comprehend living a sane, sensible, sensitive life without my commitment to God. Besides, I know that my belief works. And as a computer salesman said to a chief executive officer of a large corporation, "The fact that the computer works is proof enough that you should believe in it."

I believe in God because I choose, like most educated people I know, to listen to the advice of those wiser than myself. And Christ is still unsurpassed even among those persons whose influence in matters of religion stands out supremely in human history. And Christ believed in God. Christ prayed to him, called him Father, and claimed to be in a unique, personal, first-hand knowledge of God's reality. And any doubts I might have about the reality of God quickly lose their power when placed alongside the faith of Christ. To trust my doubts more than the faith of Jesus might well be the height of nonhumility—the ultimate display of intellectual arrogance.

If in fact God does exist, then is it possible to know him? It is possible only, of course, if God reveals himself in known and unknown laws. Science, however, leaves us with a limited perception of divine reality. The limits of science are reached when we attempt to photograph and probe spirit, and "God is spirit" (John 4:24). This means that God is morally obligated to reveal himself to the human race because of all creatures we are instinctively and incurably inclined to be religious. Only the human mind is creative enough to conceive of the grandest possibility—*the existence of God*. We humans are incurably attracted to transcendent possibility. God would be a taunting, terribly tormenting being if he left us in the dark, guessing as to what the truth really is. As Christians, we believe God has revealed himself in human form, and Jesus Christ was God's revelation of himself.

How can we know what God is trying to do in the world? The answer is found by looking at the life and listening to the teaching of Christ. He is the last Word on God's concept of human behavior. Christ is the Ideal One, for he was Self-Esteem Incarnate. And he called for the building up of a redeemed remnant of persons under his imperial leadership—a universal community of saved souls that would comprise the "kingdom of God."

What then is God trying to do in this world of ours? I believe he is trying to build a society of human beings who live out the golden rule, "Do unto others as you would have them do unto you." In modern, understandable language this means: Treat each person with dignity and respect.

This means that the kingdom of God is that invisible collection of committed Christians that transcends cultures, ideologies, nationalistic prejudices, and creeds—all bound by the golden commitment to say nothing and do nothing that would attack the self-esteem, the self-respect, and the dignity of any other human being, whether or not they are committed members of the kingdom of God. The dignity of the person then is the irreducible cell of true Christianity.

No theology of salvation, no theology of the church, no theology of Christ, no theology of sin and repentance and regeneration and sanctification and discipleship, can be regarded as authentically Christian if it does not begin with and continue to keep its focus on the right of every person to be treated with honor, dignity, and respect. At the same time, any creed, any biblical interpretation, and any systematic theology that assaults and offends the self-esteem of persons is heretically failing to be truly Christian no matter how interlaced, interfaced, or undergirded it might be with biblical references. Christ must be, at all times, Lord over the Scriptures. I cannot comprehend Christ ever treating any person, lost or saved, sinner or saint, in an insulting manner. This is not to say that the exercise of justice is out of order. (Injustice must be confronted). But when justice is meted out, it must not and need not employ a style, spirit, strategy, or substance that disregards the person's right to be treated with dignity.

God is trying to build his kingdom by appealing to our unsatisfied hunger for self-esteem. He offers to save us from guilt and shame and insecurity and fear and boredom to a life of security, serenity, stimulation, and self-esteem! Here then is a theology of salvation that glorifies God, for it glorifies his children by lifting them from hostility and rebellion-generating doubt and fear to self-confidence-building, creativity-inspiring, human-potential-releasing, human-brotherhood motivating, self-esteem. Here, too, is a theology of salvation that inspires the quality of individual life and social behavior which meets the biblical label, "Good works." As such, this is a theology that, by its nature, sustains faith, for "faith without works is dead."

In summary, what is the kingdom of God? It is a community of caring and Christ-inspired, compassionate people, who are committed to building a self-respecting society of persons whose inalienable right to self-worth controls communications, evangelism, economics, social ethics, and political systems.

Now, we turn to the second question, how in the world does God hope to succeed? "By his power." What is that? In a word, it is Christ. This is the message the church has to proclaim. It is our witness to the world. By Christ we are delivered from fear to love. We dare to love people. We are inwardly secure enough to treat everyone with respect and dignity. As such, we are not lacking in confidence so

that we have to threaten, intimidate, manipulate, dominate, control, or victimize others. Christ is our living personal friend. We are his precious associate in service, so we
need not seek earthly recognition. We are delivered from
vain ego trips and do not need to be a name dropper. All
other human connections, compliments, and credits pale
into insignificance alongside the glory of being Christ's
personal friend and ambassador.

Because of this, our self-image is dynamically positive,
for we sense that Christ's love is flowing through us. His
Holy Spirit is assuring us of our infinite worth and dignity
in his sight as we allow ourselves to be the healing channel
of Christ's nonjudgmental love. Now we see all other persons as the children of God whom Christ loves and into
whose lives he would love to dwell with grace and truth
and honor.

This position of dignity and self-worth will affect our
communication because we respect each person as a
human being. We have no right to sting another person's
dignity by unfair criticism. And we certainly have no right
to pass judgment unless we first talk to him. We must
never accuse another person in public print or speech unless we allow equal time before the same audience. We
must believe the best about others, and when we're troubled by their behavior, we must ask questions, not hurl
accusations. For example, "Do I interpret you correctly?"
"Do you mean to say or imply . . . ?" "How do you reconcile this behavior with these values I see in Christian life
and thought?"

And if after asking these questions, we are sure and
certain that the other person is completely wrong, we must
be friendly and fair as well as frank and firm with our
responses. It is at this point that we must ask the other
person, ourselves, and God *why* is he behaving in what in
our potentially erroneous judgment is unquestionably un-
Christian or antisocial behavior. And only after we have

answered the "why" will we be responsibly prepared to draft a redemptive rather than a reckless strategy to hopefully correct and convert him. I'm sure that frequently the "why" will reveal the presence of a lack of self-worth. I truly believe that further research will indicate that all "sinful," "evil," and "antisocial" behavior results from a deep emotional need—an ego-need that we can define as a hunger for self-worth. To attempt to correct an injustice or eliminate an evil or eradicate a social disease that has as its tap root a lack of self-worth, or a dignity that is unfairly assaulted, requires a skillful, noncombative approach! Tremendous skills of communication will be needed to really uproot these evils.

God's power to build a kingdom where people are treated with dignity is really the power of Christ's nonjudgmental, nonthreatening love in action for and toward people whose sins are reflections of a lack of self-esteem.

Where can we find God's power to build a society in which the self-dignity of each person is the "golden mean," the private right of each person that no one may tamper with? Or play with? Or have fun with?

God's power is Christ living in you and in me. God's power is in any person who becomes a Christian and is compelled by the love of Christ. This will affect our strategy of evangelism—we will not insult, embarrass, shame, or humiliate anyone in an effort to convert them to Christianity. We will not violate their dignity as individuals by resorting to intimidation, manipulation, or exploitation in a sincere effort to evangelize them. Instead, we will be constrained to share willingly and openly our joyous faith. And we will do so in such a time, place, and manner that they shall be introduced to our beautiful friend, Jesus. But we must be careful and sensitive not to communicate and evangelize in any way or with any words that could cause them to feel embarrassed. The style, strategy, substance and spirit of our evangelistic efforts must put a bloom not a blush upon their face.

With that spirit, we shall be effective. Evangelistic appeals to a lost soul's hunger for self-worth will produce emotionally healthy evangelists as well as emotionally healthy converts. By contrast, evangelism that appeals to a lost soul's sin and shame will stain and spoil the emotionally healthy spirit of both evangelist and convert. This explains why so many Christians continue to remain insecure, hostile, and even neurotic. A person who is converted to Christ by appeals to his need for self-respect will naturally begin to treat others with the same attitudes.

Now a theology of social ethics evolves naturally. Christ within compels us to say nothing and do nothing to lower the collectivized level of society's self-esteem.

Can we stand silent and indifferent to poverty? No, for it robs the poor of their pride as persons. Somehow we must support, inspire, or motivate the forces that can cause the poor to recover their dignity through development.

Can we stand by and allow the sin of racism? No, for it brutally strips persons of their rightful pride and leaves them feeling inferior. How can we fight this sin? We do it by recognizing that racists are fearful people. And how do we approach and convert a *fearful* person? We can do this by appealing to his pride, for once he sees himself as kind, compassionate, and inwardly secure, he will no longer perceive other races as "threats" to his own security.

The self-esteem of each person and the collective self-esteem of the community then become the holy norm, the unwavering moral north star that controls social ethics. In this kind of a theology of social ethics, we believe that any act, thought, word, or deed is sinful that lowers the collective community pride. Any behavior on our part—no matter how it may further our cause, satisfy our desires, release our frustrations, improve our lot, relieve our pain and suffering—that directly or indirectly shames or embarrasses another fellow human being then becomes unethical. That's why suicide is a sin. It's an embarrassment to the survivors. That's why war or the cavalier indifference to poverty is sinful. That is why any economic system or political system that does not permit the maximum development of the private person's possibilities is wrong! That's why a political system that maximizes human freedom is right.

Now, how does God hope to build his kingdom—his holy remnant of redeemed people in this world? I believe it is by converting persons like you and me from shame to security, from inferiority to a sense of significance, from purposelessness to purposeful living. He will use us to spread dignity to everyone we meet!

Why does God bother about it? The answer is found in the words, "For thine is the kingdom and the power and *the glory forever."*

God's need for glory compels him to redeem his children from shame to glory. God's name is glorified when his children are living honorable and glorious lives. God's glory is diminished as long as any of his children remain lost in shame, falling short of the pride and glory they should enjoy as princes and princesses of heaven. The Christian faith and life is a gospel designed to glorify human beings for the greater glory of God.

For example, the father of a family is honored and his name is honored as each of the children rise to the challenges of personal achievement—morally, spiritually, and professionally. But if just one child rejects the high call to honorable living as becomes the family heritage, the father and the family's glory is diminished.

Why should we make every effort to be as successful as we can? Why should we strive to achieve the most that we can? Why should we sacrifice to be all that we can be? Why must we build bridges? Why must we be peacemakers? Why must we compromise, again and again, in order to try to understand those who are our antagonists? The answer is simple. We must do these things so as not to stain or soil the good name of our heavenly Father whose family name we claim by his grace.

Why must we spend all of our efforts to tell the whole world about Jesus Christ? Why must we spare nothing to share the good news of each person's worth? Again, we must, because we want the entire human family to become a brotherhood and so live that we are proud of ourselves. Then, and only then will the Father be glorified.

PART III

Self-Esteem: The Universal Hope

Chapter Eleven

Self-Esteem: The Universal Hope

CAN A REFORMED THEOLOGY of self-esteem become a solid base to creatively confront the problems that face the church and the world today and tomorrow? I answer: "Yes." For at the deepest level, all social, political, economic, religious, and even scientific problems relate to the private and collective need for positive pride, or healthy self-esteem.

A major world problem since the beginning of the Protestant Reformation in 1517 is that Christian thinkers have not formulated a well-rounded, full-orbed, honestly interrelated theological system. What we need now is an integrated systematic theology that will allow for a naturally evolving, noncontrived, and nonmanipulated spawning of second-generation theological positions. The evolving theologies must reveal (not contrive) viable, nonvariable principles relating human problems beyond the salvation of a solitary immortal soul. Let me illustrate what I mean.

Some years ago I was working outside my mountain cabin repairing a roof problem. I set up a ladder, and as I climbed it, I sensed it was not too solid and was perched precariously on uneven ground. It wobbled and wiggled, but I was in a hurry and only had to spend a moment or

145

two to drive one nail so I surmised "it was okay" and "if it toppled, I'd simply jump." I was on the eighth rung when pebbles underneath the ladder's legs, like rolling marbles, threw the ladder outward and I was thrown to the ground. I broke three ribs, damaged a kidney, and spent a week in the hospital. And I learned a basic truth: *"You can't jump from a falling ladder."*

I contend that most, if not all, of the social, political, and religious problems facing our world reflect theological defects. The imperfect theology of the Protestant Reformation was really interested primarily in the "salvation of shameful, sinful, wicked, rebellious souls from eternal hellfire." Salvation was offered, very correctly, by divine grace, not by human works. When our theology started with the salvation of a human commodity called "a soul" from "hellfire," we found ourselves sincerely unable to relate that doctrine of salvation to the other human conditions that demanded theological answers.

If the primary task, from the Christian perspective, is "getting my soul saved," then, once "I've got it made," all other issues begin to seem inconsequential and irrelevant. So now "I'm saved." What's the next subject on the agenda? Racism? That doesn't relate to my salvation. I'm going to heaven when I die, anyway! So attempts by evangelicals and liberals alike to bridge economic and political issues relationally to the theology of salvation never quite connect with intellectual integrity. We have been jumping from a falling ladder!

What has happened in the history of theology might be illustrated by the following diagrams. We begin with a theology of salvation.

Now, issues arise and human problems appear on the sociological stage, but we really don't have a solid base to intellectually, ideologically, philosophically, scripturally, positively attack the problem! What are the options? Prepare a position paper against poverty or war or oppression or racism? No! The starting point, the benchmark, the sterling thread of truth, is lacking! What's the result? Something like this:

Our position seems to be that if somehow souls are saved and people are born again, society will become whole and healthy.

And we end up with a nonintegrated position like this: Disconnected theological issues arise and somehow they don't seem to be related. To someone converted to Christianity with a "salvation from hell to heaven theology," an out-of-the-blue "war-is-wrong" or "racism-is-a-sin" sermon just doesn't tie in or connect or relate to the "salvation sermon" that brought them into the Christian flock.

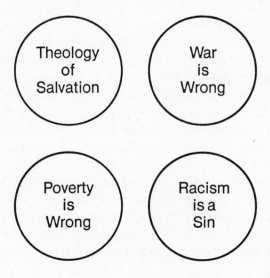

The failure of the church to redeem society after it has redeemed lost souls is more a judgment of a nonintegrated, unsystematic theology than it is the sinfulness and stubbornness and insecurity of its converts. This means that the ladder is on slipping soil, and the rungs of the ladder don't interconnect.

Result? The nation which prided itself on "great theology" saw the rise of Adolph Hitler. Meanwhile America, with all of its vital evangelicalism, found itself infected with racism. To correct these evils, the confrontation approach was successfully and painfully chosen to bring about needed change. Crisis intervention was called for because creative preventive theology had been lacking for hundreds of years.

I shall never forget some years ago while I was lecturing to church leaders in Korea that a brilliant professor of ethics excitedly approached me about my lectures on "Salvation—A Theology of Self-Esteem." He asked "Is it possible for you to develop a theology of social ethics? I earned my Ph.D. in social ethics from Columbia and while in America studied under Tillich. But even he failed at this point. He told me once, 'I don't have the theological base for a theology of social ethics.'"

The unrelated, disconnected, fractured, theologies of our century remind me of a bridge builder who starts from opposite sides of the canyon, and when both construction pieces reach the center, they miss coming together by a foot, or a mile. This illustrates how "evangelicals" and "liberals" alike have failed to come together. When you start from different points or positions the odds are that you'll fail to make connection.

"Let's build a bridge across Niagara," someone proposed nearly a century ago. Great idea, it would save miles and miles of travel and solve many problems. But how were they to begin? The canyon walls were too steep, and the rapids were too wild to get that first strand across from cliff to cliff. Then someone got a bright idea. They'd offer a ten-dollar prize to the kid who could fly a kite from one side to the other. That's how the first string got across. It was then connected to a larger string, and it in turn was connected to a slender cable. And the slender cable was connected to the strong cable that made the entire construction possible.

When the project was first announced, the critics laughed at the project. When they heard that a "kite was going to solve the problem," the sophisticated engineers had a field day. Well, history had the last laugh. One young boy, Homan Walsh, flew the first string across the chasm with his kite in 1848. He succeeded, and the process worked just as it was envisioned. The boy collected his ten dollars; the great suspension bridge was started with a single string.

I submit that self-esteem is the sterling human value that can cause a theological bridge to be built which will bring together interconnecting theologies that can positively, creatively, preventively attack the world's ills.

But can a theology of self-esteem move the mountainous social, economic, political, and religious problems today? Could a kite string make possible the beginnings of a bridge across Niagara? Yes! Only a slender string *will* succeed.

I've always been fascinated as I've stood at the rail of huge ocean-traveling ships as they approach the dock. There is no way they can come in under their own power; the momentum would assure a collision. But first, a tugboat edges the ship toward the pier. Then a sailor on the bow throws out what looks like a baseball to be caught by a dock hand. Attached to the ball is a slender cord, and attached to it is a heavier rope with a three-inch houser at the end. But only the slender cord is light enough to make the longer distance throw needed to get the "connection process" started.

A history of theology will show that we have failed because we've tried "too heavy a theology," and the connection system was never adequately designed or engineered.
Self-esteem is the silver cord, the sterling thread of truth,
that can prepare the way for a systematic theology with a
strong enough base to lead to nobler truths, loftier principles—offering creative solutions to age-old human
problems.

So I contend and plead for a full-orbed theological system beginning with and based on a solid central core of
religious truth—the dignity of man. And let us start with a
theology of salvation that addresses itself at the outset to
man's deepest need, the "will to self worth." Then we will
see how additional, second-generation theologies are
born—like healthy children from healthy parents. And in
similar fashion, each theology will affect the others.

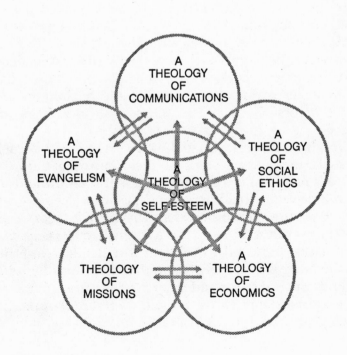

I have tried in the preceding sketch to illustrate that the Christian religion which begins with a theology of self-esteem will honestly cause to evolve, with intellectual integrity, additional related and interrelated theological systems which address the universal problems facing the human race.

I submit that an authentic theology of salvation which begins with the truth that the human being is a glorious, dignified creature, with infinite value in the sight of God, will produce a theological ladder that will stand on solid, immovable ground. And we can move up that ladder without the danger of being fashionable on the one hand or the danger of leaps in theological logic that never quite make it.

I am arguing in these pages for what might hopefully be an introductory primer for an integrated, systematic theology, positive enough to point to solutions for the problems facing the world and the church today.

It is my hope that, in these last years of the "Reactionary Age" in church history, we might be able to explore in depth and at great length the theological positions which we discuss in the following sections.

A THEOLOGY OF SELF-ESTEEM

This is, make no mistake, a theology of the salvation of the soul. Salvation is defined as rescue from shame to glory. It is salvation from guilt to pride, from fear to love, from distrust to faith, from hypocrisy to honesty. It is salvation "by grace through faith," and it is experienced when we encounter the Ideal One who accepts and does not reject us. Hence, the stronger the Christology, the richer the self-esteem; the stronger the sense of sin, the more glorious the joy of salvation and self-esteem. We were *so* bad, and yet Christ needs and wants us.

A theology of salvation that starts with an appeal to the value of the person will produce mentally and emotionally healthy human beings. At the same time, a theology of salvation that exploits the person's intrinsic guilt and insecurity can and often does produce neurotic converts.

Christians abound who are walking cases of uptight, defensive, angry, fearful, neurotic meanies. Why is this? What else can we expect if the call to conversion is a blatant appeal to a person's "depraved, unworthy, totally sinful nature"? If the seeds of evangelism are dropped in the smelly swamps of self-shame, we can expect the emerging convert, who has been "born again" in a womb of shame, to be saturated with a negative self-image. And any person who becomes a Christian without experiencing a vision of his priceless value in the sight of God will remain a blighted soul, still tarnished with a destructive, negative self-image.

Such an insecure person can be expected to project his low self-esteem in a variety of defensive reactions. He dares not admit sinlessness; consequently, the stage is set for gross hypocrisy. He or she has never really experienced "true saving grace," i.e., being accepted by a holy Jesus and treated like a prince or princess. As a result, such a person will be unable to give out what he has never taken in. He or she will demand perfection and holiness from other Christians or condemn them as either being false or "not truly born-again believers." When this happens, we are unable to be relaxed, free, liberated souls, and we remain imprisoned by the fear that we shall be exposed as a "sinner" by past or future acts.

Now we can see why there is such a lack of spiritual power in the quality of life evidenced in many church members and professing Christians today.

A professing Christian who has missed the "rebirth of a self-worth" experience will also miss the joy of love's surge through the soul. And until we sense the shower of self-love, we will be too withdrawn and unavoidably alienated from the free and happy flow of social life. Until we love ourselves (because God loves us and because Jesus Christ counts us as one of his closest, dearest friends), we will be too empty of love to give it away, and we will perceive ourselves as too unworthy to accept love from others. And the consequence will be emotionally deprived persons who are incapable of giving or receiving love.

The tragedy of Christendom today is the existence of entire congregations of church members who are dominated by emotionally deprived or emotionally under-developed persons. These congregations have been accurately labeled "God's Frozen People." Such congregations may seek collective security and attempt to bolster their united lack of self-esteem in destructive behavior. They may seek to "build themselves up" by "tearing others down." And they do this by exercising narrow authoritarianism in doctrines and practices and by sowing seeds of suspicion and dissension in the religious community.

It is true that some divisions within Christendom are the result of honest differences in theology. Yet many, if not most, of the divisions in Christendom result from deep insecurities in the minds of religious leaders. Insecure persons will be tempted to withdraw behind fences. Railings on bridges give drivers and pedestrians security, like fences in children's playgrounds offer security to the running and playing child.

So, insecure persons may be expected to bolster their faltering, feeble egos through "joining a club." And labels, which may have started out as honest definitions of theological distinctions, soon may become shields to support a collection of insecure, low self-esteeming people.

Meanwhile, the casual practice of labeling fuels and

feeds the divisive spirit in Christianity. As soon as we pin a label on a person, we produce prejudicial images which distort honest perception and make an honest perspective virtually impossible. Suspicion emerges; the possibility of trust is replaced by an attitude of fear. Every time we pin labels on people we perpetuate disunity. Confrontation and accusations replace respectful dialogue, and polarization and demeaning accusations can be expected to follow naturally. Creative communication which could build unity of spirit is a virtual impossibility.

By contrast, strong persons—self-assured personalities, whose egos find their nourishment in a self-esteem-generating personal relationship with Jesus Christ—dare to face contrary opinions, diverse interpretations, and deviations of theology without becoming disrespectful, judgmental, or accusatory.

It should be obvious, now, that in the emerging reformation the church will see psychology and theology working side by side as strong allies. The imaginary, and sometimes real, conflicts between theology and psychology should give way to creative cooperation, for no responsible, reputable school of psychological therapy disagrees with the need for people to experience self-esteem. And if theology is willing to start from the point of the person's deepest need, then both disciplines have discovered the bridge that spans the separation. Theology and psychology both need each other. In fact, classical Christian theology has for centuries been "the psychology of mankind." More than one course in systematic theology begins with anthropology—what psychology is attempting to be today, an analysis of the human predicament. Modern psychology can be extremely helpful in the analysis phase, and a theology of self-esteem can be helpful in the therapeutic phase.

The ethics of practicing psychiatry limit the freedom of

the therapist to impose his value system on the patient, but this is the Achilles heel of psychiatry. For again and again, depression, emotional malnourishment, and mental illness are caused by a patient's value system that is destructive to his self-esteem. If the pastor and the psychologist, if the preacher and the psychiatrist, are both honestly and sincerely interested first and foremost in helping a hurting soul find comfort and healing, then both will embrace each other's constructive contributions. But the bridge will be the one indivisible, nonnegotiable human need—the need for self-affirmation. Conflict between psychology and theology only means that one or the other or both have lost sight of their basic objective and have become controlled by their prejudicial dogmas instead of being committed and controlled by the crying need of a suffering human heart.

The prospects and possibilities of a church that is made up of Christians who enjoy a healthy self-esteem are really exciting. For healthy Christians do not become private clubs of God's Frozen People. Instead, congregations of persons who have a strong "I am" complex will become actively and positively involved in meeting social needs as well.

Christians who have a strong self-esteem naturally become possibility thinkers. They seek out human needs and are challenged to fill these needs. Their self-assurance is rooted in God's call. ("You have not chosen me, but I have chosen you," John 15.) They interpret this divine call to be one of commitment to serve their fellow-men. As a result, there is no conflict here between a "theology of comfort and success" and a "theology of discipleship under the Cross." For the call to "succeed" is a call to "bear fruit" (John 15:1–8). It is a call to make dangerous and daring decisions.

Possibility-thinking Christians who come out of a background of a strong self-esteem know there is no success without sacrifice. They are prepared to have their branches pruned in order to bear more fruit.

A THEOLOGY OF EVANGELISM

Since we believe that the deepest need of every person is to experience and enjoy a healthy self-respect, a distinctive theology of evangelism evolves from a theology of self-esteem. Then it follows:

1. The unconverted, the unchurched, the non-Christian is to be viewed as a nontrusting person—fearful and suspicious—instead of as an "evil" or "depraved" or "shameful" soul.

2. We must visualize every person as precious and valued in God's sight with vast untapped possibilities of service to God and his fellow-man.

3. God longs to release every person's human potential from the imprisoning, self-destructive fear and guilt that inhibits positive believing.

4. Our natural inability to trust God's love or to trust Christ's offer of salvation and forgiveness stems from our deep lack of self-worth. We simply do not value ourselves enough to believe that we can truly be loved unconditionally and nonjudgmentally. So we resist at a profoundly deep level the divine invitation to salvation "by grace." Our innate sense of shame and unworthiness compels us to believe that we have to "earn love" and "*do* something" to merit forgiveness. So, lack of trust or a lack of self-worth is the central core of sin.

5. "Unsaved souls"—insecure, nontrusting persons—will need a great deal of positive affirmation before they will be able to "listen" and "hear" and begin to comprehend the truth of saving grace. No wonder Jesus Christ employed a strategy of evangelism where he never called a

person a "sinner." They were sinners, of course, but he never *told them they were.* The proclamation of the truth of their sin would only have driven the nail of unworthiness deeper until promises of forgiveness would lack the power to loosen and extract the spike of sin, self-condemnation, and guilt.

We have a counseling center on the fourth floor of our Tower of Hope. On a certain occasion our staff psychiatrist, a medical doctor, was counseling a patient, and I had been invited to witness the session. In describing the conversation, I shall use the term "doctor" to refer to the psychiatrist and "anonymous" to refer to the patient.

This patient had a terrible guilt feeling. The doctor said: "Is it hard for you to see God as somebody who turns the other cheek?"

Anonymous: "Yes. I see God with his arms folded across his chest saying to me, 'When are you going to get your act together?'"

Doctor: "Are you perhaps confusing your mother with God?" (That was very brilliant; I mentally patted him on the back for that.)

Anonymous: "Possibly I have. Maybe I've always gotten God mixed up with both my mother and father. Maybe that's what has kept me from believing."

Doctor: "What is your mental image of Christ?"

Anonymous: "I guess as a baby. Or maybe as somebody dying on a cross. A real loser."

Doctor: "Do you think you could begin to imagine Jesus as somebody who loves you, regardless of what you are or what you've done or where you've been?"

Anonymous: "Oh, if that were possible, what freedom that would be. I would feel then that his arms were open and would come around me."

Doctor: "Can't you imagine Christ doing that?"

Anonymous: "I don't know. Why do I resist it? Why do I fight the very thing I want?"

Doctor: "You probably feel unworthy."
Anonymous: "That's it."
Doctor: "You are worthy. God was born in a manger and died on a cross for you. That means you're worth a lot to the Almighty." With that powerful affirmation of eternal truth *Anonymous* began to open up to the healing, inclusive love of God.

The most significant question that an evangelist must ask is: How can we communicate in a way that will lead a person to accept Jesus Christ as Savior and Lord? How do we convert people? By telling them that they *are* what they *are*—sinners? Or by telling them they *are* what we wish they would become? This latter technique was the Lord's approach: "You are the salt of the earth." "You are the light of the world." He understood what many of us have had to learn through lessons in modern psychology: "I am not what I think I am. I am not what you think I am. *I am what I think you think I am.*"

I shall always remember the night I was called to make a hospital call on John Wayne, the veteran film actor. He was to be operated on in the morning for what was feared to be cancer. I prayed for divine guidance all the way to the hospital. Should I come right out and ask my friend Duke Wayne if he was prepared to meet God? I was strongly led to reject that approach. Should I ask, "Are you saved and forgiven, and if you die tonight will you go to heaven?" The answer came clearly: "No, that is not what you are to say."

Then I heard the "still small voice" that I identify as the Holy Spirit of the living Christ. It said to me, "Simply bring Jesus Christ into the mind of John Wayne. He will accept or reject Christ. That is what it's all about."

When I arrived at the hospital, I found the famous actor lying on the bed clad only in his shorts. We talked, we related, and then I asked, "Duke, may I pray for you?" His response came immediately, "You bet, Bob, I need all the help I can get." I recall seeing his eyes close tightly, his rugged face taut with tension, as I prayed. Without planning or plotting or contriving to manipulate, I heard the following words come from my mouth, "Lord, John Wayne knows about you. He has heard about you all his life. He admires you. He respects you. And deep down he knows that you can and want to forgive him of all of his sins. Deep down in his mind he accepts you and believes in you and loves you, now." At that point I opened my eyes to see the face of John Wayne as possibly no other person ever saw it—peaceful as an Easter sunrise, all tension was gone. There was absolutely no evidence of embarrassment, spiritual uneasiness, or psychological discomfort. Beyond a doubt, I spoke the right words, and he followed them without resistance and with sincere acceptance.

How then do we convert and change people? We do it by the positive approach Christ himself consistently used.

In the stage play, *The Man of La Mancha*, the grand idealist, Don Quixote, meets a harlot named Aldonza. "You will be my lady," he announced to the shock of this whore. Then he added, "Yes, you are my lady, and I give you a new name—Dulcinea." She laughs scornfully.

But Don Quixote followed the approach Jesus used with Mary Magdalene. Undaunted, he keeps affirming her and declaring her to be what he wants to believe she is. And, of course, the affirmation becomes a self-fulfilling prophecy.

The play continues and the stage is empty. It is night. Offstage a woman screams. It is Aldonza. She is being raped in the hay. She appears onstage, hysterical, blouse torn, hair disheveled, dirt on her face, terror in her eyes, breasts heaving with the fast breathing of a panic-stricken soul. Loud and clear comes the voice of the Man of La Mancha, "My lady!" She can't handle this and screams, "Don't call me your lady; I was born in a ditch by a mother who left me there naked and cold and too hungry to cry. I never blamed her. I'm sure she left hoping that I'd have the good sense to die."

Aldonza is weeping now, head downcast, humiliated, shame-wracked. Then her shame turns into violence, and as her head rises, she screams, "Oh, don't call me a lady. I'm only a kitchen slut reeking with sweat. A strumpet men use and forget. Don't call me a lady; I'm only Aldonza. I *am nothing at all!*" She then whirls and runs into the night, but Don Quixote calls after her with a loud voice, "But you are *my* Lady Dulcinea!"

The curtain drops, but shortly it rises again to the death scene of this glorious dreamer of the impossible dream. He is dying now, like Jesus, of a broken heart—scorned, laughed at, despised, and rejected of men. Suddenly, to his side comes what appears to be a Spanish queen in a mantilla and lace. She kneels and prays. He opens his eyes and asks, "Who are you?" "Don't you remember?" The lady rises and stands tall. She is beautiful, perfectly proud and perfectly humble at the same time. She speaks softly, "Don't you remember? You called me your lady. You gave me a new name. My name is Dulcinea!"

The conversion was complete! She was born again!

In summary: a theology of evangelism not based on a theology of self-esteem may be judged unethical, unhealthy, and ultimately unsuccessful if it manipulates, intimidates, or humiliates a human being in the process of trying to convert a person.

Bill Bright, founder of Campus Crusade for Christ, told me once: "When I was converted, I was converted not out of a consciousness of sin, but I was attracted to the love of God in Christ. . . . Once I ran to receive him as my Lord I became, in his presence, strongly aware of my sin and imperfections, and I was genuinely repentant." "Sinners" dare to repent in the presence of Christ whereas they will "fear" repentance in the presence of their fellow imperfect human beings.

6. The gospel of Christ must be proclaimed as salvation from shame to glory, from self-doubt and self-condemnation to self-confidence and self-affirmation. Now we are released to become creative, healing, and redeeming persons.

A Theology of Social Ethics

If we start with a theology of self-esteem, and employ a theology of self-esteem-generating evangelism, the bridge will be built for a natural theology of social ethics to evolve. And this provides us with an answer to the following question: Is it possible to develop a theology which can authentically dissolve the classic tension between "The Social Gospel" and "The Gospel of the Salvation of Souls"?

The answer is yes, if we begin with human dignity as the primary, basic, ultimate human value. "Pride of sonship" was the joy of Adam. Shame was the result of "The Great Divorce" between God and our first parents. Glory restored is the real fruit of salvation. A compulsion to love, i.e., to treat all persons with the dignity they deserve as human beings, is the natural compulsion of the true born-again Christian. If conversion results in a salvation experience, a dissolution of guilt, and a rise of self-esteem, then the Christian will be constrained by the love of Christ and controlled by a compulsion to treat persons beautifully. We have to "put out" what we have "taken in."

If a theology of self-esteem is the starting point for evangelism, a theology of social ethics built on human dignity is as natural as breathing. Then any social act which insults another person, demeans another human being, oppresses another person's possibilities, lowers to any degree the collective level of social self-esteem, or retards the development of community pride is a violation of the theology of social ethics that the kingdom of God demands from a true disciple. And that is a sin, no matter how it satisfies my desire, fuels my prejudices, relieves my frustration, eases my pain, fulfills my ambitions, furthers my goals, or climaxes my lusts.

The classical error of historical Christianity is that we have never started with the value of the person. Rather, we have started from the "unworthiness of the sinner," and that starting point has set the stage for the glorification of human shame in Christian theology. The strong and not incorrect Protestant emphasis on "salvation by faith, not by works" resulted in hundreds of thousands of "anti-good-works" sermons. And the result has produced an incurable contradiction between the theology of salvation and any contrived theology of social ethics. For this reason, an authentic theology of social ethics in classical, evangelical theology became an impossibility.

A theology of social ethics that rises from a theology of self-esteem will attack the *root* of racism. Victims and propagators alike are gradually, but surely, healed from this social evil. Racism, oppression, war, and violence are all healed naturally, albeit indirectly, and hence more effectively, for this natural process avoids the inflammatory approach which only alerts the "enemy" to set up defenses. What, after all, is the root cause of racism? Racism is the defensive reaction of a fearful, non-self-esteeming person. So, racism is to be understood as stemming from a deep problem that is really based on insecurity or fear. And "fear" is the face of a soul that lacks "trust."

How do we change—*redemptively*—angry, fearful people? We do it by "being as wise as serpents and as harmless as doves." The absence of this approach casts light on the pitiful record of the Christian church as it relates to the social injustices in society. We might well argue that we have failed because the successes we can point to are few, limited, and tragically tardy. And no branch of religion, no sect of Christendom or Judaism, can claim any honors.

Why is our record so shameful? I believe it is for these reasons. We have tried to tackle the evils in the wrong way. Ministers and clergy were told to "preach sermons," "condemn the sins," "be daringly prophetic," and "take up your cross." But the result has offered limited success, inadequate achievements, and many a bloodied congregation.

Is there a better, wiser way? I say, "Yes." It is by disarming the racists until they no longer feel threatened, and victimized. The social sins are too deeply rooted in our culture to ever be corrected by the direct head-on-clash approach. To be positively prophetic calls for far more wisdom, patience, insight, and even agape.

Back in the 1950s the American church was suddenly alarmed over an extremist political group. Pastors were asked to preach sermons on a given Sunday against this "evil" group. The edict was carried out. The bloodbath was painful in more than one congregation where the non-extremists, who had friends and neighbors among the extremist group, were shocked at the angry sermons from their "beloved pastor" who suddenly was seen as a "mean minister" attacking a patriotic relative.

I chose a different strategy. I said to the ministerial association: "There are two ways to fight a wolf. First, make sure that it is a wolf and not someone's German Shepherd! Then, once you're sure it's a wolf, you can go on the attack. You may win or you may lose. But if you win, you may earn the admiration of everyone.

"Another tack is possible: Build large fires and remove all food—the true wolf will drift away from the light and move on to where he can be fed, or he will die of starvation." I chose this latter approach.

I analyzed what was really dangerous about *some* of the members of the extremist group and then launched into a

series of sermons entitled "Believe the Best about People."
A few of the extremists, whom I analyzed as serious neu-
rotics, left the church. They were emotionally hungry for
sermons that could fuel their appetite for fear and suspicion. However, many "conservative" persons who were in
the group or were about to join it were positively conditioned and matured into responsible and beautiful church
members. This way I didn't kill tender young flowers
while trying to root out the weeds.

THEOLOGY OF ECONOMICS

The next step on our theology ladder is a theology of
economics, simply because poverty remains a central, social, worldwide blight. I believe there is hope that we might
be really fresh, creative, and futuristic, even by being realistic, in finding an exciting answer to the question: "Can a
progressive, positive, nonreactionary theology of economics be developed that will unite disagreeing factions in
Christendom? Again, the answer is yes if our starting point
has been with a theology of self-esteem.

Perhaps no social issue is more basic on a world-wide
scale than the problem of poverty. Many thinkers believe
that it is the basic cause of war. Thoughtful persons from
widely divergent economic philosophies must find a solid
base, a ladder of understanding, that can allow us to build
a fresh Christian theology of nonreactionary economics
based on the deepest human need.

We have discovered that the sting and sin of poverty is
shame, and we can agree that to tolerate poverty is a violation of a theology of social ethics committed to building
pride in persons. A theology of self-esteem lays the foundation for a theology of economics that can bring together
sincere Christians on the right and on the left of the classical economic spectrum. Only extremists who are neurotic

reactionaries or destructive revolutionaries would reject participation in dialogue.

Since this is true, let us now look closely on the emerging universal economic principles that would highlight our theology of economics.

I submit the following principles as guidelines to a theology of economics that rise from a theology of self-esteem.

1. Human dignity must be recognized at the outset as the noncompromisable human value in attacking the poverty issue.

2. The loss of self-esteem must be seen as the real plague and plight in poverty. What makes real poverty a human tragedy? It isn't the absence of material comforts or pleasures. Rather, it is the oppression that poverty bestows: the loss of freedom to develop the self-dignity-generating possibilities and discover the self-worth-inflating options which release people to pursue the pride-producing alternatives in life.

3. A cavalier attitude of indifference toward poverty cannot be allowed by either the rich or the poor without contributing directly or indirectly to the lowering of the collectivized level of community self-respect.

4. We must reject any suggested solution to the poverty problem that oppresses or manipulates the poor while it promises them material survival.

"Man shall not live by bread alone," (Matt. 4:4, RSV). The end does not justify the means. We must remain vigilant against the subtler, sophisticated, economic imperialists sometimes disguised as elitists. The intellectuals do little to build the self-esteem of the common man, while elitists promise solutions, but do not offer self-esteem to simple persons.

Totalitarianism of the right or left cannot and must not be accepted as "a necessary transitional stage." For history proves that power corrupts and absolute power corrupts absolutely. The love of and the lust for power sustains such a stranglehold in every oppressed society that abdication of this evil never occurs voluntarily. Intentional perpetuity of power is inherent in every form of tyranny.

5. We must reject all solutions to the poverty problem that provoke either physical or verbal violence. The shame of bloodshed quickly absorbs whatever pride or glory might be offered in a victorious war. Our will and resolve must be strong enough to believe that we can achieve economic *compatibility* without yielding to *combatability*. Violence cannot be tolerated. "I don't want to be dead to get ahead," commented a poor person in South America.

6. We must seek a solution that maximizes individual freedom while it liberates the person from poverty's chains. Change, not chains, must be the goal. The economic philosophy with dignity and freedom offers every person the opportunity to believe in himself; develop himself; dream daring dreams; make private personal decisions; pursue risks (i.e., practice faith); succeed and be self-affirmed; fail and become a wiser and more self-reliant person; prosper and accumulate an estate (small or large); invest in human service-oriented enterprises; become financially independent from social, civil, or corporate control and enjoy true economic liberation; and, finally, the freedom to give it all away to persons or projects he or she may select in godly conscience. Let no solutions deprive any person of the glorious dignity-generating experience that comes with the joy of voluntary giving.

7. We must seek to create solutions that motivate, inspire, and challenge persons to see and seize their individual possibilities. We must be on guard against falling for solutions that stifle human initiative. We must not be blind to the self-esteem-suffocating effect of antipoverty proposals that serve the power and ego goals of opportunistic politicians more than they serve the deepest needs

of the poor. One of the hardest jobs in the world is to find a way to give money without doing more harm than good to a person's pride.

8. Our theology of economics must be based on an infinite faith in the human potential based on the Judeo-Christian doctrines of creation and providence. Our economic theology will be carefully crafted and contrived to prod and produce the noble "Incentive Impulse." The handicapped, whether physically, mentally, emotionally, economically, racially, culturally, or educationally handicapped, must all be perceived as still pregnant with undiscovered and undeveloped possibilities. No effort must be spared to inspire them to believe in themselves, for again, the "I am" will determine the "I can." Any economic theology that fails to inspire personal progress and individual growth will fail to feed the person's deepest need—the pride of personhood. And as such, it fails to pass the final exam of all theology—it simply does not glorify God. The economic theology that stimulates the successful and sanctified exploitation of human possibilities glorifies the God who created the person. Possibility thinking, then, is the pathway to human pride and, hence, the glory of God. God is not glorified so long as his children live in shame; it is impossible to glorify God until we glorify his children.

If for whatever reason we withhold an economic handout, it must be coupled with this believable challenge, "I believe in you. I believe you can do it. I see you succeeding in your strength and God's." It is this kind of a faith in people that can produce a self-fulfilling prophecy.

9. We should pursue positive, creative, antipoverty proposals that aim at creating job opportunities which challenge the person to develop his or her untapped potential and learn the most valued of all human possessions—pride of achievement.

10. Finally, our theology of economics—based on the nonnegotiable commitment to every person's pride—must be a theology that is sensitive and responsible to community.

John Crean was living in a state of spiritual and economic poverty when a wise friend said to him, "John, there are two kinds of people—losers and winners, takers and givers. Takers are losers; givers are winners. If you want to win, you have to stop taking and start giving. Give more to your boss on the job; give more than is expected from you. Then see what happens." It was radical advice, but he followed it. He was noticed and rewarded. John saved enough to start a business "built on the giving, not taking principle." He decided to manufacture a product that would really solve deep human needs—he'd provide job opportunities to persons who could enjoy the pride of earnership. He'd offer a financial package so poor people could afford to buy and enjoy the pride of ownership.

The result is history. He succeeded and became financially independent and wealthy. Now, he has just given thirty percent of his capital base toward development of a retreat and renewal center where the poorest of the poor can find freedom from their oppression. And who are the poorest of the poor? They are people who have lost all faith in themselves, in the positive potential of society, in God, and in their fellow-man.

The issue today is far deeper than socialism versus capitalism or an equal distribution of wealth. Rather, the central issue is the generation of human pride.

A truly constructive, creative theology of economics must avoid solutions that suffocate motivations to self-development and must produce a "theology of incentive impulse." Surely, a religion that fails to inspire a noble incentive impulse in the human spirit cannot be judged to be truly creative and productive and functionally wholesome.

A THEOLOGY OF COMMUNICATION

A theology of self-esteem that contends for the dignity of persons sets the stage for, and urgently demands, a theology of communication.

If the church is losing members, it must mean that either we have an unnecessary product, or we are offering a service no one needs, or we are representing an unacceptable, nonviable cause. In my judgment it is none of the above. Instead, we are losing members because we are very ineffective communicators.

The truth is: we have never bothered to articulate a "theology of communication." While riding the high horse of autocratic authority, we simply make our royal pronouncements. Roman Catholics utter their Papal edicts, Protestants quote their Bible, Fundamentalists declare their orthodox theological dogmas, and we are all expected to renounce private reflection and peacefully acquiesce to these pronouncements. And the result is that the dignity of the person is violated by such oppressive, intelligence-smothering forms of communication. But the need of people for respect and dignity is so great that they will not be taken in by such pronouncements—they will just abandon the camp.

A theology of self-esteem will give rise to a theology of communication where the following principles cannot be ignored.

1. We are ill-prepared to speak or write until we can communicate our viewpoints in positive words and in a respectful manner that carefully considers the dignity of the audience.

2. The fulfillment of the important role of critic does not give us the license to be unfair, insulting, or embarrassing in method, manner, or mode of communication

3. The setting and the stage must be carefully considered and crafted before controversial issues are discussed. Any

subject that is controversial implies that intelligent persons hold contradicting interpretations. The setting and stage must, therefore, allow for the freedom to question, challenge, and dialogue. The inherent dignity of a person is violated when his free spirit is oppressed or manipulated. So, an autocratic announcement or unchallengeable authoritative argument on controversial issues offends the intellectual pride of listeners.

Controversial subjects—political, social, theological, or debatable biblical interpretations—should be handled in a classroom setting where the person feels comfortable and free to mentally explore all intellectual options without the demeaning oppression of intimidation by a faulty and imperfect preacher or professor.

One classical role of the pulpit in Protestantism has been to "preach sermons" which imply indoctrination more than education. Within this form of communication, there is an inherent, intrinsic inclination to intimidate, manipulate and, hence, offend the person's most prized quality of humanness—his dignity. The style and spirit and substance of the sermonic form of communication did not fail the church in a society which was conditioned to accept the authoritarian approach. Persons who were born, reared, and trained in societies accustomed to the rule by royal decree or Papal pronouncements or cleric commands accepted a certain mental attitude of intellectual and emotional serfdom.

From this soil there arose the pulpit, the preacher, the sermon. Then came the rise of societies that valued freedom and educated children to recognize and respect the duty and right to express contrary opinions. In America we have been exposed to the self-esteem-generating right to sincerely disagree. No wonder, then, that Americans will resent any form of communication that offends our freedom of conscience.

4. If the self-esteem of a person is the highest value,

then a theology of communication leaves little if any room for sarcasm.

To use sarcasm and irony as literary devices without insulting and embarrassing defenseless victims, who are not granted equal time and space on the same platform, is almost impossible. We cannot and must not violate any person's right to be treated with dignity.

In a theology that starts with an uncompromising respect for each person's pride and dignity, I have no right to ever preach a sermon or write an article that would offend the self-respect and violate the self-dignity of a listener or reader. Any minister, religious leader, writer, or reporter who stoops to a style, a strategy, a substance, or a spirit that fails to show respect for his or her audience is committing an insulting sin. Every human being must be treated with respect; self-esteem is his sacred right.

The freedom to be critical must not be viewed as a license to be sarcastic and destructive. Our freedom to be critical stops at each person's right to be treated with respect. If in the critical process we contribute to any person's inferiority complex, we are destructive. It is essential that we constantly remember that every human being is a person for whom Jesus Christ died on the cross—*now we know what God thinks of us.*

5. No matter how right my cause or how true my position, I must not make negative statements about other people unless I will give them equal time before the same audience. If this is not humanly possible and I still feel I have the right to be critical, I must make every effort to inform them of my intended remarks and offer the opportunity to correct my possible misunderstanding of their position, protecting both them and me from the embarrassment of promoting inaccuracies.

6. We shall be constantly conscious that until we are able to verbalize our cause and concern in positive terms, we may become our own worst enemy. It is most difficult to

crusade for a cause without doing it more harm than good. To arouse negative passions is the most dangerous way to attack an evil. The toll in terms of emotional destruction is almost always too high a price to pay. More often than not the crusader may enjoy personal relief from frustration; he may even win the admiration of supporters for his courage to carry his cross. But the pragmatic question must be faced: Did he succeed? And did he manage to win converts? Or did he only destroy an enemy? And did he manage to protect innocent people from being battle casualties?

My father was an Iowa farmer. Every spring he would send us out into the fields in a declared war against cockleburs. We chopped them, dug them out, burned them and fought them with chemicals. But they managed to survive until my father planted alfalfa. This marvelous "food-for-milk-cows" crop sends roots twelve feet deep. The growth was so thick that the cockleburs were crowded out.

The reformation that must happen in today's church will not be complete until we learn to communicate by pushing people's green buttons and stop hitting their red buttons. We have succeeded when we are able to use that form of communication which stimulates the positive emotions of faith, hope, love, humor, courage, and optimism.

The world is waiting to rush to hear the good news of Jesus Christ—if it is positive, not negative; polite, not rude; kind, not cutting; inspirational, not inflammatory; constructive, not destructive; clean, not dirty; beautiful, not ugly.

A THEOLOGY OF MISSION

Finally, a refreshing, exciting, enthusiasm-generating theology of mission emerges. For real mission is meeting human needs. And in the process, we shall see secularism sold short by a bigger, better, and more beautiful idea—positive Christianity. We won't need to fight secular humanism; we simply offer a deeper, more desirable alternative. For no philosophy, no ideology, no theology can meet the deepest needs of human beings as attractively and pragmatically as a dynamic and dignity-instilling Christian theology of self-esteem.

We hear a great deal these days that we live in "one world." The ability of nations to launch nuclear missiles that will reach Chicago or Moscow or Peking or London in thirty minutes has caused thoughtful people to realize that we human beings are "all on the same boat." Oil shortages and high-level international finance has caused an interdependence to evolve between nations that would have preferred the luxurious isolation where "locked-in thinking" could prevail. But that day is gone forever.

Satellites, jet travel, oil, gold, dollars, missiles—all point to realities that remind intelligent rational people that all of us are passengers on the same plane—a flying craft called "planet earth." And we all use the same oil, breathe the same air, drink the same water, and consume the same proteins. We're all in the same craft flying through space at the speed of 24,000 miles per hour.

True, the captain and the officers may never meet or mix with those who handle the maintenance of the craft. And the first-class passengers may never get acquainted with those traveling economy class. There may be a dozen or more "communities" within the ship. These "communities" may be estranged or strangers, but all are on the same craft. And whenever a defect or a rupture appears on the craft, every last person will be affected until the defect is repaired. I submit that the entire human race is on the same craft and it has a defect—lack of self-esteem. And this defect will give rise to a dangerous pride that could cause the ship to crash.

For over a quarter of a century I have been writing, lecturing, listening, and trying to discover what might become a universal, unifying human need. And I have found that all cultures, civilizations, races, and ethnic groups reflect a profound need for self-worth. It takes different forms, wears different masks, presents different faces, but at the very core of the human soul is a need for self-esteem.

We've all heard the labels that are applied to people: Jews are "stiff necked"; Germans are stubborn; the French are haughty; English people are proud; Americans are also proud; Orientals "can't lose face." Admittedly, these are generalizations, but, most assuredly, they point again and again to the same deep need for every person to be "affirmed." All of these human characterizations relate at the deepest level to the need for self-esteem. On the other hand, destructive pride, what the Bible labels a sin, is a lack of that humility which comes when we experience a sense of our infinite value at that moment when we know we are loved and forgiven unconditionally by God in Jesus Christ. Real self-esteem is real humility. Healthy pride and honest humility are the same human qualities—just different sides of the same coin. We all welcome affirmation and resent being insulted.

I believe that today we are witnessing the last days of the Reactionary Age in church history. And I'm further convinced that we are witnessing the birth of a new Age of Mission. I can readily imagine that a professor of church history teaching in a theological seminary in the year 2300 would outline the history of Christianity as follows:

The Apostolic Age	The Church Age	The Great Schism & Dark Ages	The Reactionary Age	The Age of Mission
Christ's death to 100 A.D.	101 A.D. to 999 A.D.	1000 A.D. to 1516 A.D.	1517 A.D. to 1999 A.D.	2000 A.D. to the present day

The sixteenth-century Reformation will be seen as a reactionary movement. (It was necessary; even the Roman Catholic Church has admitted this.) And the period from 2000 A.D. on will be labeled as the Age of Mission.

How shall we launch the new Reformation? It will come as we listen to and learn from Jesus Christ. What the church desperately needs are Christians who are genuinely "discipled." Christians who learn to live under the discipling discipline of the Lord's Prayer until we find healing from the self-esteem-destroying emotions and become good communicators of a healthy gospel. Then we shall live out a successful theology of mission. And we shall see a new church emerge in the next century—a body of believers who are relaxed, confident, inwardly secure people. The 2000th birthday of Christ could mark the end of the Reactionary Age in church history (1517–1999) and inaugurate the Age of Mission—Christ's church born again!

What power for missions this will release! Yes, here is a theology for church growth. Here is a theology for success, for the secret of success is to find a need and fill it. Truly, when the church reforms and refines all of its theological expressions around every person's daily need for self-affirmation, it shall flourish "like trees planted by rivers of water."

The church structure which houses the congregation which I serve as the pastor is called The Crystal Cathedral. It is well recognized as a work of art. This, too, is the result of a theology of self-esteem. Great art should bring pride to the human family. Ten thousand "little people" contributed twenty dollars a month for twenty-five months to "buy a window" to "honor a loved one," and, together, ten thousand nonfamous people felt pride in building something beautiful for God.

As the construction of the Cathedral with glass walls and

ceilings neared completion, I was pressed by many around me to compose words to a dedicatory hymn appropriate to the occasion.

The words of that hymn sum up a theology of mission that rises from a theology of self-esteem.

> People, people, everywhere,
> Each a jewel fair and rare.
> Wake up, world, lost in fear;
> Jesus calls to hope and cheer.
>
> People, people, round this earth
> Hunger for a deep self-worth.
> See the Cross. The holy sign.
> Shape your life by this design.
>
> Be a window—let all see
> Christ within you living free.
> Be a mirror to reflect
> Dignity and self-respect.
>
> People, people, will you dare
> Venture forth in noble prayer?
> Claim your heritage divine!
> Born to be a star to shine!
>
> People, people, trust God's dream
> That can feed your self-esteem.
> Christ will build your life anew.
> God loves you, and I do, too.
>
> Christ my Savior help me see
> This grand possibility.
> Saved from sin's indignity!
> Saved to love eternally.

Notes

Introduction

1. Author of, *Feeling Good: The New Mood Therapy* (New York: William Morrow & Co., 1980).
2. *Celebration of Life,* copyright © 1981 by Rene Dubos. Used by permission of McGraw-Hill Book Company.

Chapter One

1. R. C. Sproul, *Stronger Than Steel: The Wayne Alderson Story* (New York: Harper and Row, Publishers, 1980).

Chapter Six

1. "Trust and Its Consequences," *Psychology Today,* Oct. 1980.

Chapter Eight

1. *U.S. News and World Report,* Sept. 9, 1974.